"Erica Lagalisse's *Occult Features of Anarchism* is a wonderful and learned provocation. Taking the concept of modern politics as a form of theology and magical ritual, she traces some aspects of the origins of socialist and anarchist politics and performance to the Hermetic tradition that influenced the Radical Enlightenment and its originators, in, for example, the work of Spinoza. But she also argues that this "magical" or Hermetic tradition rested on a masculinist coup against women's knowledge, especially in the transformation of women healers into malevolent witches. This work, however, is not merely a work of academic research. Lagalisse then argues that the gatekeeping behavior of anarchist and radical militants in the global justice movement, the Occupy / Square movements, and their more recent spin-offs reproduce the masculinist guardians of the esoteric knowledge of the Freemasons and other secret societies that draw directly or indirectly on the Hermetic tradition. Thus, forms of "indigenous" knowledge in the Global South and the widespread popularity of conspiracy theories in the Global North are belittled, ignored, and not engaged to the peril of the left's emancipatory project. Lagalisse applies to the concepts of cultural capital and indirectly the New Class a new and interesting synthesis."
—Dr. Carl Levy, professor in the Department of Politics and International Relations at Goldsmiths, University of London, and author of works including "Social Histories of Anarchism," *Journal for the Study of Radicalism* (2010)

"*Occult Features of Anarchism* is an engrossing read that hijacked my attention from start to finish. Lagalisse excavates the theological, spiritual roots of anarchism to identify some of the contemporary shortcomings of left activism. Engrossing, enlightening, and often surprising, the book delights and dazzles as it ruminates on a stunning array of topics from gender and intersectionality to secret societies, the occult, and conspiracy. A must read for those interested in the history of anarchism, rethinking the role of secrecy in revolutionary movements, and emboldening anarchist organizing today."
—Dr. Gabriella Coleman, professor of anthropology at McGill University and author of works including *Hacker, Hoaxer, Whistleblower, Spy: The Many Faces of Anonymous* (2015)

"This is surely the most creative and exciting, and possibly the most important, work to come out on either anarchism or occultism in many a year. It should give rise to a whole new field of intellectual study."
—Dr. David Graeber, professor of anthropology at the London School of Economics and Political Science and author of works including *Debt: The First 5000 Years* (2011)

"A tour de force. Any self-respecting radical should know this history, right down to the dirty history of the A-for-anarchism sign from its origins within Freemasonry to its association with magic. Ripping apart with historical detail our contemporary common sense we learn the tactics of how elite radicals claim power through difference. The significance of this history for the politics of now should not be underestimated and should most certainly be more widely known. Essential reading."
—Dr. Beverley Skeggs, director of the Atlantic Fellows program at the International Inequalities Institute of the London School of Economics and Political Science and author of works including *Class, Self, Culture* (2004)

"Lagalisse deftly demonstrates the gendered qualities of anarchism and how these have been undertheorized. Trained as an anthropologist, she applies her astute ethnographic eye to a historical study of the left, unearthing the development of classical anarchism and socialism within private brotherhoods defined by gendered exclusion, yet granted as the "public sphere" of politics. Her study of anarchism as a historical object complements her previous ethnographic studies of the "public" and "private" taken for granted within today's anarchist social movements, for example, her essay "Gossip as Direct Action" (2013). Fun and fascinating, playful and serious at once, *Occult Features of Anarchism* further reveals why and how the social worlds of the left often carelessly reproduce and even further entrench mainstream forms of gendered power."
—Dr. Sally Cole, professor of Anthropology Emerita, Concordia University, and author and editor of works including *Contesting Publics: Feminism, Activism, Ethnography* (2013)

Occult Features
of Anarchism

K A I R O S

In ancient Greek philosophy, *kairos* signifies the right time or the "moment of transition." We believe that we live in such a transitional period. The most important task of social science in time of transformation is to transform itself into a force of liberation. Kairos, an editorial imprint of the Anthropology and Social Change department housed in the California Institute of Integral Studies, publishes groundbreaking works in critical social sciences, including anthropology, sociology, geography, theory of education, political ecology, political theory, and history.

Series editor: Andrej Grubačić

Kairos books:

Practical Utopia: Strategies for a Desirable Society by Michael Albert

In, Against, and Beyond Capitalism: The San Francisco Lectures by John Holloway

Anthropocene or Capitalocene? Nature, History, and the Crisis of Capitalism edited by Jason W. Moore

Birth Work as Care Work: Stories from Activist Birth Communities by Alana Apfel

We Are the Crisis of Capital: A John Holloway Reader by John Holloway

Archive That, Comrade! Left Legacies and the Counter Culture of Remembrance by Phil Cohen

Beyond Crisis: After the Collapse of Institutional Hope in Greece, What? edited by John Holloway, Katerina Nasioka, and Panagiotis Doulos

Re-enchanting the World: Feminism and the Politics of the Commons by Silvia Federici

Occult Features of Anarchism: With Attention to the Conspiracy of Kings and the Conspiracy of the Peoples by Erica Lagalisse

Autonomy Is in Our Hearts: Zapatista Autonomous Government through the Lens of the Tsotsil Language by Dylan Eldredge Fitzwater

The Battle for the Mountain of the Kurds: Self-Determination and Ethnic Cleansing in the Afrin Region of Rojava by Thomas Schmidinger

Occult Features of Anarchism

With Attention to the Conspiracy of Kings and the Conspiracy of the Peoples

Erica Lagalisse

K
KAIROS

PM

Occult Features of Anarchism
Erica Lagalisse
© 2019 PM Press.

ISBN: 978-1-62963-579-8
Library of Congress Control Number: 2018931523

Cover Image: Mixed media collage by author, 2017. The collage features images from the Rosicrucian Manifestos (*The Temple of the Rose Cross, Teophilus Schweighardt Constantiens*, 1618), Tommaso Campanella's *Civitas Solis* (City of the Sun, first edition, 1623), Laurence Dermott's rendition of the *Masonic Arch* (1783), the "Pyramid of Capitalism," popularized by the Industrial Workers of the World (circa 1911), as well as designs and artwork by Giordano Bruno, William Blake, and others less famous, including a fragment from the zine *Anarchism and Hope* by Aaron Lakoff (Montréal, 2013).
Cover by John Yates / www.stealworks.com
Interior design by briandesign

10 9 8 7 6 5 4 3

PM Press
PO Box 23912
Oakland, CA 94623
www.pmpress.org

"Well, a 33rd degree Freemason lying on his deathbed once told me the great secret, and you know what it is? 'Christ was just a man,' he said."

—*Roy Wright (1941–2018)*

May he enjoy wandering the phantom library of Alexandria, chatting up the angels.

Occult Features of Anarchism

An Initial Treatise
On the Liberatory Cosmology of Western Anarchism
The Relation of *Socialism* and *Pantheism*
&
The HERMETIC TRADITION
in Modern Politics
(attending to
both the
Conspiracy of Kings
&
Conspiracy of the Peoples)
With Relevance to Current Struggles Against
TYRANNY
And Practical Challenges of Coalition Politics
in the 21st Century

By

Spartacus Tonans
Supreme Magus of the Kitchen Garden, 007°
AKA
Erica Lagalisse

London
2019

Contents

Foreword
by Barbara Ehrenreich

I first came across Erica Lagalisse's byline about four years ago
and was so impressed by her work that I promptly tracked her
down. Not many young intellectuals were as acutely sensitive
to class issues as she was, and by class I don't just mean the 1%
versus the 99% but the seldom discussed boundary between
college-educated professionals and blue-collar workers. The
first time she wrote to me she seemed wary to the point of being
suspicious. Maybe she was wondering whether I was one of
those snooty hotshot feminist academics she had encountered
along her way to a PhD, and, if so, what did I want from her?
Soon enough though, we were engaged in a lively correspondence about everything we were working on and thinking about.
Drafts of articles were exchanged, along with copious links
related to politics, popular culture, and philosophy. In due
time, we met and spent long evenings theorizing over dinner
and wine.

She is a feminist and leftist like me but closer to anarchism, and at a demonstration more likely to be found with
the direct action crowd than in the tamer precincts where I
hang out. In many ways though, we're very similar—both children of working-class parents and familiar with class-based
insults as well as sexist ones. We'd both encountered misogyny
on the left, which had led to some strained relationships with
our male "comrades." And we're both curious about everything and willing to drop whatever else we're doing to learn
something new. In no time at all, I was editing her writing and

helping get it published, while she was encouraging my more reckless speculative tendencies.

Erica has been working on this book in one form or another for as long as I've known her. At first her motivation seemed impenetrably esoteric to me: Why would anyone want to trace the tangled roots of modern left-wing thought back to their origin in distinctly "irrational," even mystical, ways of thinking? Gradually, I began to see the deeper question here: What kind of authorities do we listen to and who do we ignore? What makes one kind of person credible and another dismissable? In modern Western culture, the accepted authorities have tended to be white males with extensive formal educations. Hence the female indigenous health worker introduced early on here barely gets a hearing from Erica's male anarchist comrades, because, as a religious person, she is not "rational." And clearly she is not male.

Another disturbing incident occurs among the anarchists, this time including Zapatista supporters from Mexico. They are sitting around talking about the seemingly invincible power of governments when the conversation wanders to secretive organizations like the Freemasons and the Illuminati. This surprises Erica, who has so far encountered these organizations only on YouTube. But it gets worse: one of the people involved in the conversation points out that the hypothesized secret organizations are dominated by Jews. Erica is shaken; after all, the speaker is a self-proclaimed revolutionary and by virtue of participating in this mixed-nationality discussion a de facto internationalist, and hence "cosmopolitan," a label traditionally applied to Jews. She makes the obvious empirical objections, which are eventually accepted. But meanwhile Erica is forced to confront her own ignorance. Neither she nor the professors at her university had ever paid any attention to the conspiracy theories that explain social injustice to so many people.

At this point you may be expecting a learned diatribe against conspiracy theories, with their fanciful origins and dangerous tendencies toward scapegoating. But hold onto your seat: Erica is far too subtle a thinker and far too intellectually restless to fall for a convenient shibboleth, even one almost universally endorsed by prominent liberals and left-wingers. Instead she throws herself into the study of YouTube films that "document" everything from the U.S. government's role in the 9/11 attack to the plot to assassinate John F. Kennedy—and not in order to debunk these theories (others have already put plenty of effort into that) but to assess their appeal. Certainly, in a world where so little *is* certain, where elections can empower the enemies of democracy, and even the weather is increasingly unstable, it's satisfying to point out that powerful and well-organized people are in charge.

Pointing out that conspiracy theories are often as not the intellectual property of the working class—the class that cannot usually afford the kind of education that would lead a person to reject them out of hand—she argues that the elite prejudice against such theories is just another facet of the elite prejudice against working-class people themselves. All right, conspiracy theories lack the intellectual and scientific trappings of academically respectable theories, but they also have a certain explanatory advantage. The elite theories—in, say, the social sciences—attribute causation to vague "systems" and "forces," most of which are invisible to the untrained eye. Why, for example, do the poor remain in poverty, while the rich get richer all the time? Because of the "system," the forces that hold the majority of people down while propelling a tiny minority into unfathomable wealth. The appeal of a conspiracy theory is that it replaces these invisible, almost mystical, entities with actual people, even if they include such unlikely suspects as the Knights Templar or the Rothschilds. Who is chosen as a target here may be cause for serious argument, but of course a general search for those responsible is appealing and understandable. When injustice is being perpetrated, it's good to know the names of the perpetrators—and probably their addresses as well.

In the U.S., the association between conspiracy theories and the white working class was strengthened by Trump's victory in 2016. Despite data highlighting the role of higher income people in electing him, mainstream pundits blamed his success on poor whites, typically those who had lost their jobs to deindustrialization. With Trump came a raft of conspiracy theories, beginning with his own favorites: the story that Obama's presidency was illegitimate because Obama is actually a Kenyan. Right-wing radio host Alex Jones added others: the government is controlling the weather; a pizza restaurant in Washington, DC, houses a Democratic child sex trafficking operation; Satanists are taking over America. There are reasons why so many liberals and leftists use the term "conspiracy theory" in a strictly derogatory sense.

But just because so many conspiracy theories are right-wing lies doesn't mean that there are *no* possible conspiracies that we ought to take seriously. The combined efforts of foreign policy experts, journalists, and politicians to promote the notion that Saddam Hussein possessed weapons of mass destruction may be counted as a "conspiracy." So too, perhaps, can the events leading up to George W. Bush's dodgy election in 1999. When I talked to a noted political scientist about the role of conspiracies in history, she was silent for a moment, and then said that she wished she had heard this years ago, because there are so many events that hint at possible conspiracies—like the serial assassinations of liberal and radical leaders in the sixties (the Kennedy brothers, Martin Luther King, and Malcolm X.) But she knew that that line of thought had been closed to respectable academics.

Be warned: this is a challenging book, one that sent me off to Google page after page. But it's been worth every bit of the effort. There are no boundaries here between academic disciplines or, when you reflect on it, even between centuries. Like my social scientist friend, I found it powerfully disinhibiting, inviting me to think in ways I had always rejected and toward conclusions I had never imagined. You will have a similar experience. Young as she is, Erica Lagalisse has given us an exhilarating lesson in how to think and a what a politically involved person should think about.

Introduction

The year 2006 was a dramatic one in Mexico. Protestors in Atenco were violently attacked, raped, and imprisoned. The people of Oaxaca rose up against the governor and successfully barricaded the state capital for months. President Calderón took the election, although most were certain López Obrador had really won (and a new phase of paramilitary war promptly began). I spent most of the year in my hometown Montréal, Canada, yet was paying close attention to all this as a member of a Zapatista solidarity collective.

The Zapatistas, for those unfamiliar, are the indigenous rebels who staged an uprising in the southern Mexican state of Chiapas on January 1, 1994, coinciding with the inauguration of the North American Free Trade Agreement (NAFTA). They were the first resistance movement to effectively make use of internet media, which was novel at the time, to call for a global mobilization in support of their cause and against neoliberal capitalism in general. The Zapatistas strongly appealed to a new generation of leftists who were disenchanted with the fallen state socialism of the Soviet Union, yet also unsatisfied with liberal "rights" politics as an alternative: the Zapatistas were not seeking to take state power, but their politics were strongly anti-capitalist. For over a decade, championing the Zapatistas was very much "the thing to do." The Zapatistas were so influential that their gathering in Barcelona in 1998 drew a huge crowd of international activists who went on to organize the People's Global Action network, which convened the large protests in Seattle and elsewhere that marked the turn of the millennium, and which came to be known as the "alterglobalization" or "global justice" movement.[1]

The Zapatistas had been lying low in the early 2000s but made a sensational reappearance in early 2006. Parallel to the electoral campaign that year, the Zapatistas toured the country seeking to inspire a nationwide anti-capitalist resistance movement. According to the latest of the Zapatistas' seductively florid communiqués, those of us beyond the borders were invited to take up the cause as well, and thus form part of the Zezta Internacional. And so it was, in Montréal in 2006, that about twenty of us had formed a Zapatista collective. The group was mostly Mexican but included a few Québécois like me. For a while we were all very close. One day when some of us were sitting around chatting after a collective meeting, one member lamented how our efforts were insufficient. We had organized demonstrations, raised funds for political prisoners, and arranged transnational speaking tours, but we were still terribly ineffective compared to those in power. "Those guys," he said, "are extremely fucking organized."

"What do you mean?" I asked, because he had suddenly spoken in a quiet, ominous tone, as if referring to something beyond the obvious fact that presidents have big armies with tanks and we don't.

"Their cooperation is international, and beyond that of governments. The higher-ups have allegiances to one another

1   Regarding the Zapatista rebellion and its international influence, see, e.g., Neil Harvey, *The Chiapas Rebellion: The Struggle for Land and Democracy* (Durham, NC: Duke University Press, 1998); June Nash, *Mayan Visions: The Quest for Autonomy in an Age of Globalization* (London: Routledge, 2001); Alex Khasnabish, *Zapatismo Beyond Borders: New Imaginations of Political Possibility* (Toronto: University of Toronto Press, 2008). I discuss the Zapatista movement in more detail and provide further references in Erica Lagalisse, "'Good Politics': Property, Intersectionality, and the Making of the Anarchist Self" (PhD diss., McGill University, 2016).

that supersede any notion of national interest. They have rituals that bring them together. They are drunk on their own power. They know the secrets of magic and are fucking us all with methods of mind control." I asked more questions, curious about these sensational claims, especially the part about magic. The three people in the group who apparently shared these views proceeded to explain. Their conversation meandered around the topics of international trade agreements, global banking, the Knights Templar, and Freemasonry. They often disagreed among themselves as to the details. I wasn't familiar with the stories they were telling. Some of it sounded plausible. When one of them added that the powerful global elites in question were all Jewish, two of us stopped him. We proceeded to debate: even if there are secret ritual fraternities decorating the capitalist class, is it really reasonable to think they are all of one religious persuasion? Isn't it more believable that the allegiances among these "higher-ups" supersede questions of religious as well as national identity? That we all suffer under the global system of economic exploitation as we do, because powerful capitalist Christians, Jews, Muslims (and others beyond) act in their collective interest as capitalists more than anything else?

The question was not to be settled in the space of an hour. I walked away somewhat shaken. I would have to figure it all out. I decided I would familiarize myself with this Freemasonry business, read the sources they had recommended. Next time, I would have an informed argument prepared. One had mentioned a book called the *Protocols of the Elders of Zion*, which I promptly ordered off the Internet. I also tried looking up Freemasonry on YouTube, which was a brand-new media phenomenon at the time. Before long, I was spending two hours every evening watching videos on the secret order of the Illuminati, legends of the Sphinx, and how the Fibonacci number series is built into the architecture of sacred Egyptian buildings.

3

The stories were entertaining, and as an anthropologist it was fascinating to observe how the novel social technology of YouTube encouraged the viewer to consume certain videos on the basis of others recently viewed, thus inviting further connections of meaning (semantic links) among and within video contents. When, in 2007, I attended a local anti-war march and beheld participants holding placards with images of Egyptian pyramids topped with eyes, yet all inverted to suggest a power structure being turned upside down, I suspected where these demonstrators were getting their ideas. I realized I was conducting an (auto)ethnographic research project, being at once the viewer of YouTube videos and the viewer of my own and others' YouTube viewing: Why did people find some videos more seductive than others? What were the narrative and cinematographic devices that effectively appealed to my own (racialized, gendered, classed) subjectivities? I found John Anthony West's series on Magical Egypt amusing, but why? Did the eccentric, bearded white man in the safari outfit evoke the familiar authority of a BBC documentary? Was it his performance of citation (however disorganized), mimicking the academic genre, that I enjoyed? Was it the aesthetically pleasing symmetry of his geometrical diagrams?

Meanwhile I continued to discuss the question of global conspiracy with my friends and comrades, now fully aware of the contents of the *Protocols of the Elders of Zion*, as well as the genesis and social history of this text, which has played a special role in anti-Jewish propaganda since the early twentieth century. Readers may be relieved to hear that I did eventually convince the comrade who had recommended this book that powerful capitalists and Jews are not one and the same. Rhetorically, I had to grant that there are, or at least may exist, opaque global organizations of powerful men beyond the obvious and publicly admitted ones (such as the World Trade Organization, the United Nations, etc.), and in turn he granted the likelihood that such opaque organizations would contain men of different national and religious backgrounds. (As for magical mind control, we'll come to that later in the book.)

The story might have ended there, in 2008, two years after it began. I had satisfied my curiosity and purpose. I had also become entirely absorbed in my PhD and happily left the charged quagmire of confusion about Freemasonry and the French Revolution behind. Yet a number of things happened, each independent from the other, which brought me back to my once informal studies. We might even playfully suggest that the universe conspired.

First, activist responses to my past academic work analyzing anarchist collaborations with indigenous peoples' struggles and how anarchists' gender bias and atheism both get in the way of "solidarity" efforts encouraged me to articulate in more detail the gendered history and cosmology of classical anarchism.[2] In this previous publication, which was based on fieldwork I had done for my master's degree in anthropology, I described how a group of anarchists working in different activist collectives, including our Zapatista collective mentioned above, collaborated to organize a speaking tour of two indigenous activists from Mexico throughout Quebec and Ontario, Canada.[3] I then analyzed the events of this well-intentioned tour to illustrate various unacknowledged forms

---

2   This past work is Erica Lagalisse, "'Marginalizing Magdalena': Intersections of Gender and the Secular in Anarchoindigenist Solidarity Activism," *Signs: Journal of Women in Culture and Society* 36, no. 3 (2011). Note also that for purposes of citation, the academic reader may wish to refer to the peer reviewed rehearsal of the present work, Erica Lagalisse, "Occult Features of Anarchism," in *Essays on Anarchism and Religion*, vol. 2, ed. Alexandre Christoyannopoulos and Matthew Adams (Stockholm: Stockholm University Press, 2018).

3   Beyond Lagalisse, "Marginalizing Magdalena," the reader may also look to Erica Lagalisse, "Gossip as Direct Action," in *Contesting Publics: Feminism, Activism, Ethnography*, ed. Sally Cole and Lynne Phillips (London: Pluto Press, 2013) for an account of our Zapatista collective's activities and internal politics, as well as a more detailed story of the speaking tour.

of racism and sexism in constructions of "anarchoindigenist" solidarity work among white (settler) solidarity activists. Within this particular ethnographic case, Montréal anarchists had marginalized the voice of the indigenous woman activist Magdalena during her speaking tour, due to a combination of gendered and racial prejudice.

During speaking events, Magdalena tended to recount stories about her experience as a community health worker (*promotora*), describing how government representatives tried to persuade her to promote sterilization among indigenous women in the region. Magdalena also spoke of the need to maintain harmonious ways of life among the communities (*pueblos*) and the need to respect all of Creation—land, water, animals, and people. According to many anarchist audience members, she did not have an "analysis" since she situated her struggle in religious as opposed to political and economic terms, while she also displayed less "experience in politics," because she had not participated in "union movements," but rather worked against the forced sterilization of indigenous women—a distinction based on gender. Each of these prejudices would have worked against her independently, but the overlapping effect of two public/private dichotomies (as applied to sexuality and religion) made it especially difficult for her listeners to understand her as political. In my essay I elaborated how this conjuncture was no coincidence. Secularization in the West privatized religion during the same historical process and by way of the same logic that it privatized the sexual.[4] The coincidence of "public versus private" discourse as applied to both the domestic/political and religious/secular dichotomies in anarchist politics thus relies on a gendered order. The disqualification of religion from the modern left and its feminization

---

4   On this point, see also Joan Scott, "Sexularism," in *RSCAS Distinguished Lectures* (Florence, IT: European University Institute, Robert Schuman Institute for Advanced Studies, 2009).

were one and the same, with each dichotomy serving to rein-
force the other. I suggested that more attention to both current
and historical correspondences of secularism, colonialism,
and gender could benefit both scholarship on left politics and
contemporary anarchist solidarity activism.

Following the publication of that article, responses by
both academic and anarchist activist readers held to a certain
pattern. Most were happy to admit that we must "pay more
attention to gender," generally speaking, and regarding my
question of anarchist atheism, many agreed that we should
indeed be more "respectful" of "indigenous identity." This last
continually disturbed me, as I had taken care to emphasize that
the problem goes beyond a failure to be sufficiently polite in
the presence of difference. Beyond being "disrespectful," the
modern Western insistence on a mechanical universe delimits
the radical imaginary in general.[5] To refrain from telling the
non-atheist activist they are wrong (while continuing to think
they are), simply because he or she is a person of color, is altogether different than deconstructing one's colonial mentality,
which treats the religious as Other in the first place.

In short, I returned to the drawing board partially to
further elucidate this point. In the previous piece, I had
emphasized that it was in the context of the colonial encounter
that Christendom granted other communities and traditions
the name it had only ever given itself—religion—and reincar-
nated itself as "secular."[6] Now, however, I would also hold up
for detailed examination the specific metaphysical premises

5   See Lagalisse, "Marginalizing Magdalena," for elaboration of this
    argument with reference to, e.g., Talal Asad, *Formations of the Secular:
    Christianity, Islam, Modernity* (California: Stanford University Press,
    2003); Gil Anidjar, "Secularism," *Critical Inquiry* 33, no. 1 (2006);
    Gloria Anzaldúa, *Borderlands / La Frontera: The New Mestiza* (San
    Francisco: Aunt Lute, 1987); Jacqui Alexander, *Pedagogies of Crossing:
    Meditations on Feminism, Sexual Politics, Memory, and the Sacred*
    (Durham, NC: Duke University Press, 2005); Joan Scott "Sexularism."
6   See especially Gil Anidjar, "Secularism."

embodied in modern Western definitions of "politics" and the theology of modern "revolution," so that anarchists would understand that they have a cosmology too.

In the course of my subsequent studies, I discovered much to my dismay that any inquiry into the gender of the modern revolutionary left that digs back farther in history than the union movements of the masculine wage-working proletarian (the classical anarchist movement per se) necessarily stumbles upon the institution of Freemasonry, among other clandestine fraternities. Was it wise, I wondered, to highlight the association of anarchism with charged topics like Freemasonry, given all of the intrigue I had recently witnessed on YouTube about "secret societies" and their role in contemporary politics? Besides, I was already a rather isolated feminist in my academic department, quickly becoming known as "the anarchist" as well (in spite of the fact that my scholarly work is critical of "anarchism"), and was also somewhat stigmatized among my peers due to my working-class background. If it were to become known that I was studying Freemasonry alongside all of that, I might lose my tenuous grasp on respectability.

A year later, however, when writing my final PhD qualifying essay on the history of anarchism, my tutor and chair of the McGill University history department, Dr. Catherine Legrand, encouraged me to complement my study of nineteenth- and twentieth-century syndicalism with a focus on classical anarchism's roots in nineteenth-century theosophy and Freemasonry. I began to accept my fate.

Ultimately, I decided that it was not only practically responsible but politically necessary to publicly broach the thorny topic of the clandestine revolutionary society. By 2012, even a quick check back on the thriving contents of YouTube confirmed that stories about "Illuminati" Freemasons secretly crafting a "New World Order" and controlling both "right" and "left" political movements had become significantly more prevalent than in 2006 and were enjoying increasing numbers of "views." Many videos reporting that the attacks on the World Trade Center in New York on September 11, 2001 were an "inside job" were now also linking this specific alleged conspiracy with that of the "Illuminati." David Icke's YouTube videos that linked the U.S. Occupy movement (circa 2011–2012) with Jewish lizard-men bent on destroying humanity were watched by thousands upon thousands of viewers, whereas no documentary made by actual Occupy participants had enjoyed nearly so large an audience. I began sharing concern among friends and colleagues, who sometimes exchanged nervous glances in response, as if merely mentioning knowledge of YouTube videos on the "Illuminati" was enough to relegate me to an embarrassing realm of intellectual invalids. I tried to explain that while respectable researchers may insist that popular "conspiracy theories" of power are laughably false, these cultural productions may nonetheless contribute to real political effects, such as the growing neofascist movements in North America, which are not laughable at all. When Donald Trump won the U.S. election in 2016 and professional middle-class liberals realized that "conspiracy theorist" pundits such as Alex Jones had been enjoying more credibility than they for quite some time, I was depressed but not surprised.

The neofascist ("alt-right") movements in the United States do enjoy a significant amount of support from persons who enjoy theories of global power involving Freemasons, Illuminati, and Jews, all popularly referred to as "conspiracy theory." Precisely on account of so much disinformation regarding the revolutionary fraternity in popular culture and its real-world effects, it may be politically useful to clarify the record on these topics—an ambitious project, to which this little book is but a modest contribution. I do hope readers make use of this essay in such a practical way.

Here, skeptics may counter that there is simply no point in trying to critically engage "conspiracy theorists" in reasoned conversation, as the "conspiracy theorist" (thus reified as a particular type of person) is by definition irrational. In North America in 2018 it is also common to hear both radical and liberal elites suggest that persons are only attracted to "conspiracy theory" if they are already hopelessly anti-Semitic and strongly attached to other forms of racism. The folk sociological account of "conspiracy theory" hegemonic among the professional class further suggests that "conspiracy theories" are only attractive to small-minded people looking for a simple and therefore satisfying explanation for global exploitation and violence (although many proposed "conspiracy theories" are not particularly simple). The "conspiracy theorist" is also imagined to be politically apathetic: the idea that global capitalism is headed by magic-wielding aliens means there is no use in organizing against it. In short, according to many educated elites, "conspiracy theorists" are all thirty-something white men who live in their mothers' basements (a euphemism for working-class status) and are socially unengaged except for periodic ranting on their respective keyboards. And if "conspiracy theorists" tend to be white working-class men, this is because only people who benefit from race and gender privilege in society would need to invent an imaginary wizard caste of evil world leaders to explain why economic developments don't seem to be working out in their favor.

The many YouTube videos I have reviewed over the years are, by and large, presented by disaffected white men, and surely this last suggestion above reflects certain insight. And I too have had many conversations with "conspiracy" buffs who do not play by the rules of logical argument, and for whom my university studies on the topic merely prove that I am an untrustworthy element of the "Illuminati" establishment. Yet my studies originally began because of an argument I entertained with educated Mexican men who were active members of a Zapatista collective—they were not white, nor were they politically apathetic, and while one of them was originally attached to anti-Semitic stories about modern banking, following debate he considered altering his theory of history. With this in mind, one wonders if progressive elites themselves are not being somewhat irrational, or perhaps holding on to a crude stereotype of "conspiracy theorists" as a way of justifying a comfortable routine of disengagement, wherein the English-speaking world is increasingly ridden with anti-Semitic theories of global conspiracy but it's "not worth trying" to change anyone's mind. Of course, reasoned debate will not be sufficient to turn devoted neo-Nazis away from their project, but it may affect the future actions of those still sitting on the fence, so to speak. And maybe when it comes to fighting fascism, every possible strategy is worth trying.

The following historical exposition is therefore presented with a dual purpose, and, accordingly, two distinct analytical discussions conclude the book. The penultimate chapter revisits the questions of gender and the secular in relation to settler anarchoindigenism that I originally posed in my first aforementioned essay. Having now explored in detail the hidden correspondences between classical anarchism, Renaissance magic, and occult philosophy, Western anarchism appears more obviously a historical product, whose genesis within clandestine masculine "public" spheres of the radical Enlightenment continues to inflect anarchist understandings of the "political" even today. By illustrating the cosmology of classical anarchism, I complicate present-day anarchist attachments to "secular" analyses, in which anarchist theology is simply displaced and mystified. By attending to the same story, we witness the coevolution of modern masculinity and secularized social movements as a textured historical process. We observe the privatization of both gender and religion in the praxes of radical counterculture, which develop in complex dialectic with the "privatization" of gender and religion by the modern nation-state.

The same discussion allows us to historicize gendered, racialized anarchist notions of "sovereignty" and "autonomy" and consider the implications of such definitions with respect to practical efforts to challenge diverse forms of domination within social movements and in the world at large: while charting instances of "anarchy" throughout time and space may be a valid political project, there is also much to be gained by charting the emergence of "anarchism" as a distinct "ism"—and to do so does not necessarily detract from the aforementioned project, but rather keeps us honest as we proceed.[7] It is one thing for anarchists to maintain that they are "against all forms of domination" nominally speaking, yet a decolonized anarchism that properly challenges gendered power requires acknowledging how the secularization of social movements against the state mirrors the secularization of the modern colonial state itself, which privatizes religion and gender yet continues to embody a specific cosmology and patriarchal arrangement in both structure and ideology. Put bluntly, "conspiracy theorists" may sometimes be stubborn white men, but then again so are anarchists, who may be attached to some frustrating ideas about power as well.

The final chapter then presents a preliminary ethnographic analysis of "conspiracy theory." As charting the construction of the secret society (both real and imagined) in European history has increasing practical political import, within this final discussion my historical exposition is (re) presented as having specific pedagogical utility for political activists and scholars of the left who may wish to critically engage the challenge(s) of "conspiracy theories." For example, my presentation of the objective history of the Illuminati allows us to observe the curious fact that many contemporary popular theories surrounding the "Secret Order of the Illuminati" presume that this group has actually achieved the ends of its historical adversary, the Holy Alliance—or as it was

7   On this point, see also Carl Levy, "Social Histories of Anarchism," *Journal for the Study of Radicalism* 4 (2010): 8–10.

known in the nineteenth century, the "Conspiracy of Kings"—
wherein it becomes important to ask: How, why, and to what
end has this confusion come to pass? We also revisit certain
questions briefly presented in this introduction, analyzing in
more detail, for example, how "conspiracy theory" as a label
(discursive category) is mobilized to garner or challenge class
respectability. With attention to an exemplary ethnographic
case—an argument about "Jewish bankers" on an Occupy
Wall Street listserv—I suggest the need to explore how activists' opposing arguments on either side of "conspiracy theory"
debates are defined by a priori premises regarding history
and causality, and how these appear related to differences of
class subjectivity.

Any study of "conspiracy theories" raises questions of
epistemology, in which all ideas stigmatized as "conspiracy
theories" are not equal; some fail reasonable tests of rationality, others do not. Given that the phrase "conspiracy theorist"
is, in the majority of cases, applied to working-class people,
in theory educated activists who aspire to "take lead" from
oppressed subjects might wonder if popular theorists may be
offering certain positioned insight. The Illuminati is not in
control of world government, nor are Jews in control of the
banking system, yet is it also wrong to posit the ruling class as a
"conspiring" to destroy us? Does the U.S. Food and Drug Agency
really have the public's interests at heart? Are people really
wrong to suspect the government and its agencies of conscious
malevolence? Bourgeois professional associations arguably
constitute a class-based and class making conspiracy in and
of themselves. The fact is that all politics involves "conspiracy," whether "from above" or "from below." Perhaps, as in the
case of my own original argument with my Zapatista friend,
it would be expedient to grant certain rhetorical ground to
the "conspiracy theorist," for the sake of critically interven-
ing in particular theories of "conspiracy" where and when it
matters most.

For practical pedagogical purposes such as these, I have explicated my sources very clearly. At times my lengthy footnotes may appear eccentric, yet given how both the internet and published print are saturated with sensationalized accounts of "secret societies" and related intrigue, which makes it difficult for either lay or academic researchers to penetrate the historical record surrounding these phenomena, I purposefully present this work as a bibliographic essay of sorts, useful for the student who wishes to investigate further. The reader will notice that I often offer multiple sources in reference to a given point, sometimes explaining briefly the character, approach, or historical context of each one, as well as the non-English sources to which the authors refer to in turn: much of the relevant primary material and reliable scholarly secondary sources with respect to the clandestine revolutionary fraternities is not in English. According to my own skill set, I have not reviewed the German and Italian sources as much as I have the French- and Spanish-language works, yet in the course of my essay I do make an effort to provide the reader with a non-exhaustive list of important non-English-language sources and clearly indicate the relatively scarce English-language scholarship on the topic of Freemasonry and other clandestine fraternities and the historical relation of these to classical anarchism.

All of this being said, it is explicit that I come to the historical studies at hand methodologically as both an anthropologist and for the purposes of practical intervention within social movements and politics today. It is from being a participant (2000–2005) and later an ethnographer (2005–2015) within contemporary anarchist social movements that I consider it important to unpack the history of "anarchism." I purposefully engage the past from the perspective of the present, tacking back and forth between diverse times and places to unearth bits and pieces of buried anarchist history based on an ethnographic imagination, using both secondary and primary sources. The interdisciplinary activity necessarily involved in such a project means that diverse specialists will hopefully be inspired to add some qualification, and thus lend their own knowledge and methodological strengths to the problem. Strangely, or perhaps not so strangely, the particular metaphysics of modern anarchism and its relation to social and historical context has not so far received the attention it deserves. This is no doubt partially due to the bias of many anarchists against religion, and the bias of many scholars against anarchism, but is perhaps also because the topic requires delving into the relationship between anarchism, occult philosophy, and "secret societies"—all charged topics, even independently. As explained above, at first I resisted engaging the subject, yet I was increasingly called upon to try. May my readers approach the work generously and forgive certain necessary gaps within such a short, accessible book about such a large, inaccessible topic.

First Premises: The Theology of Politics

Carl Schmitt's general point that modern politics embodies secularized theological concepts is of basic relevance here. Schmitt remarks, while pursuing his particular question regarding sovereignty, that every political idea "takes a position on the 'nature' of man," presupposing that "he is either 'by nature good' or 'by nature evil,'" and that to "committed atheistic anarchists, man is decisively good."[1] This essay will dovetail with Schmitt's summary remark in only some ways; for our purposes a more nuanced discussion of the transcendence versus immanence of divinity in the history of ideas within Western philosophy is crucial. I am inclined to point to Marshall Sahlins's work on "The Sadness of Sweetness: The Native Anthropology of Western Cosmology."[2] Sahlins suggests that the theological preoccupations underlying European political theory and science can be traced back at least as far as St. Augustine and the quarrel of pagan, platonic, and gnostic positions with that of the emerging Church authorities regarding the transcendence versus immanence of divinity, i.e., whether nature and humanity, together or separately,

---

1   Carl Schmitt, *Political Theology: Four Chapters on the Concept of Sovereignty* (Cambridge, MA: MIT Press, 1985), 56.
2   Marshall Sahlins, "The Sadness of Sweetness: The Native Anthropology of Western Cosmology," *Current Anthropology* 37 (1996): 379–418. (The particular history of ideas offered below was first presented to me in the form of David Graeber's lecture notes from Dr. Marshall Sahlins's theory seminar, ca. 1990.)

are wholly, partially, or latently divine, or are merely borne from the divine.

Cast in Sahlins's light, the persistent dualist conundrum in Western politics and social theory appears as a spiraling repetition of this same theological concern: there is Lust, which is not of God; there is Matter, distinct from Spirit; there is Desire, as opposed to Reason. Those who suggest some coercive force stops (or must stop) us from pursuing our "animal" desires follow the logic of a transcendent divinity. Since we are by nature so evil and base, God—or something else "out there" conceptually derived from Him—must keep us in line. For St. Augustine it was the state of Rome, for Hobbes any sovereign will do (his "self-interest" clearly evolving from Augustine's "desire"). The "individual" vs. "society" polarity evident in most social theory is only another manifestation of the same—here God becomes "society" (rather than "the state"). One could go further and point out, for example, that in Émile Durkheim's work the transcendent force appears as the "social fact"—from a mass of pre-social individuals and desires emerges "society," which then serves to restrain these desires.[3] Furthermore, note that in methodological individualism desire creates and governs society, whereas in cultural determinism desire creates the society that then governs desire, but it is always the same terms in play. In short, the transcendent God of theological dualism can be found just beneath the surface of every argument for centralized authority, including most canonical social theory (which anarchists, we may note, tend to recognize as "authoritarian").

What if we approached modern "antiauthoritarianism" with the same lens? I propose that a particular theological thread likewise runs through it. The same cultural baggage in tow, developing in dialectic with its opposite, modern

---

3   See, e.g., Émile Durkheim, *The Rules of Sociological Method*, (Glencoe: Free Press, 1966 [1895]).

antiauthoritarianism grapples with the same theological dilemma, yet attempts to resolve it differently by rearranging the terms and with recourse to various pagan traditions and syncretic Christian hereticism itself. In other words, whereas many have located "anarchist" elements in Christian millenarianism and non-Western traditions, I wish to draw attention to the latter as elements of "anarchism" itself. Modern anarchism has never been purely atheist except in name, and instead develops based on overlapping syncretic pagan cosmologies that behold the immanence of the divine. In fact, utopian socialism, anarchism, and Marxism each rely (in ways both similar and different, which I will tease out below) on a specific syncretic cosmology that is incipient in the Middle Ages, changing and crystallizing in the Renaissance, and gradually given a scientific makeover throughout the Enlightenment up to the twentieth century. Just as the secularization of the modern state privatizes religion and sexuality but continues to embody a particular theology in its structure and ideology, the social movements that resist this dominant power structure go through a similar process of secularization in parallel, wherein gender and religion are likewise displaced from "politics" (as above, so below).

A Heretical Account of the Radical Enlightenment

Standard histories of modern anarchism often locate its precursors in the heretic movements (e.g., Anabaptists, Ranters, and Diggers) that articulated combined critiques of Church authorities, the enclosures of private property, and forced labor during the feudal period and early capitalist order.[1] These movements often called for communal ownership in Christian idiom, for example, by elevating "grace" over "works," yet the form and content of these heretical social movements was different from the Christian millenarian movements that preceded them.[2] Millenarian movements were spurred on by a charismatic individual or momentous event, whereas the heretical movements had defined organizational structures

---

1   See, e.g., Peter Marshall, *Demanding the Impossible: A History of Anarchism* (London: Fontana Press, 1993); Atindranath Bose, *A History of Anarchism* (Calcutta: World Press, 1967); George Woodcock, *Anarchism: A History of Libertarian Ideas and Movements* (Cleveland: The World Publishing Co., 1962).

2   See Bose, *A History of Anarchism*; Christopher Hill, *The World Turned Upside Down: Radical Ideas during the English Revolution* (Harmondsworth: Penguin Books, 1975); Peter Linebaugh and Marcus Rediker, *The Many-Headed Hydra: Sailors, Slaves, Commoners, and the Hidden History of the Revolutionary Atlantic* (Boston: Beacon Press, 2000); Silvia Federici, *Caliban and the Witch: Women, the Body and Primitive Accumulation* (New York: Autonomedia, 2004); Peter Burke, *Popular Culture in Early Modern Europe* (Cambridge: Cambridge University Press, 1978); Norman Cohn, *The Pursuit of the Millennium: Revolutionary Millenarians and Mystical Anarchists of the Middle Ages* (Oxford: Oxford University Press, 1970).

and programs for change. The heretics aspired to a radical democratization of social life by reinterpreting the religious tradition against the interests of the institutional Church and broader established order, developing both a wide network of schools and safehouses, leading at least one historian to call them "the first proletarian international."[3] What does it mean that anarchist historians easily recognize such movements as "anarchist" when they are located safely in the past—as "precursors"—yet as soon as modern anarchism proper is articulated, religious levelling movements are seen as backward, if not heretical to anarchism itself?

The shift from the spontaneous millenarian movement to the organized heretical one and later to the secularized "proletarian international" proper had much to do with the dissemination of diverse mystical doctrines that began circulating in Europe during the Crusades. Platonic philosophy, Pythagorean geometry, Islamic mathematics such as algebra, Jewish mystical texts, and Hermetic treatises were all "rediscovered" via Muslim Spain and translated into Latin during this time. It is well known that the creative recomposition of this ensemble inaugurated the Renaissance and later the "Enlightenment" on the level of high culture, but how the composite led to new levelling projects from below has received less attention. The Hermetica in particular is largely unrecognized as a fount of modern left politics, yet is an important thread running through it. We therefore do well to briefly consider the Renaissance magician before further engaging the Enlightenment and the radical Enlightenment in turn.

---

3   Federici, *Caliban*, 33. See also Cohn, *Pursuit of the Millennium*; Henry Charles Lea, *A History of the Inquisition of the Middle Ages* (London: Macmillan, 1922); Malcolm Lambert, *Medieval Heresy: Popular Movements from the Gregorian Reform to the Reformation* (Oxford: Basil Blackwell, 1992); Walter L. Wakefield and Austin P. Evans, *Heresies of the High Middle Ages* (New York: Columbia University Press, 1991).

The Hermetica or *Corpus Hermeticum* is a collection of texts written in the first or second centuries A.D., yet during the Renaissance they were held to be the work of Hermes Trismegistus ("Thrice Greatest Hermes") imparting the mystical insights of ancient Egypt. Egypt was held to be an "original" and thus superior civilization, one that nourished the philosophy of the Greeks, for example, such that the discovery of these texts was especially prized. When a monk arrived in Florence from Macedonia in 1460 carrying some of the Hermetic texts, Cosimo de' Medici ordered his translator to drop Plato's dialogues immediately and turn his attention to them.[4]

The Hermetic tradition beholds a unified universe of which man is a microcosm ("as above, so below"), and wherein cosmic time beholds a pulsation of emanation and return. The Hermetic cosmos is hierarchically arranged in symmetrical diachronic and synchronic bifurcations (dyads) and trifurcations (triads), but a web of hidden "correspondences" and forces—alternately "energy" or "light"—cut across and unify all levels; in duration everything remains internally related—"All is one!" Significantly, humanity participates in the regeneration of cosmic unity—our coming to consciousness of this divine role is a crucial step therein. God and creation thus become one and the same, with the inevitable slip that our creative power—including intellectual power—is divine. The creative power of the Word (the Logos) is given particular attention, often spoken of interchangeably with the sun, "second god" or demiurge. Divine creation first inheres in the luminous Word, and man the microcosm may create in turn. Of course, the initiate must first purge himself of false knowledge in order to be

---

4   See Frances Yates, *Giordano Bruno and the Hermetic Tradition* (Chicago: University of Chicago Press, 1964), 12, passim. For the Corpus Hermetica itself, see Brian Copenhaver, *Hermetica: The Greek Corpus Hermeticum and the Latin Asclepius in a New English Translation, with Notes and Introduction* (Cambridge: Cambridge University Press, 1992).

able to receive the true doctrine; at any given moment only some are ready. Hermes himself explains that he "keeps the meaning of his words concealed" from those who are not.[5]

The Hermetica has proved adaptable to a variety of projects. Its neat metaphysical geometry, which arrived alongside algebra, Euclid's "Elements of Geometry," and the Pythagorean theorem, helped form a composite that lent itself to a massive investment in mathematical forms and understanding. Mathematics became the hidden architecture of the cosmos, the most permanent and basic truth, and revelation of these secrets certainly did permit an ability to build and create in ways never before imagined—providing both vaulted cathedrals and calculus, for example. A variety of mystical doctrines proliferated from the interaction of this composite with preexisting natural philosophy, alchemy being only the most famous. Hermetic logic can also be discerned in a variety of other eclectic doctrines that developed throughout this period, such as Joachimism, Eckartean mysticism, Paracelcism, the mathematics of John Dee, the Lullian arts, Rosicrucianism, vitalism (followed by spiritualism, mesmerism, and more), all of which behold secret cosmic "correspondences" and sacred geometry. Frances Yates illustrates how the features of Hermetic metaphysics find place, for example, in the *magia naturalis* and sun worship of Marsilio Ficino (1433–1499), the Christian cabala of Pico della Mirandola (1463–1494), the occult philosophy of Cornelius Agrippa (1486–1535), and the metaphysics of Renaissance and Enlightenment figures to follow,

---

5   The quotation is from *Corpus Hermeticum* 16, cited in Copenhaver, *Hermetica*, 58; see also Yates, *Giordano Bruno*, for substantial detail of Hermetic metaphysics, including the status of the Word or Logos within (the *mens, intellectus* / Word, *anima mundi* have been rendered as / from the Christian Trinity in multiple ways throughout the history of the Renaissance); see 151–6 for specific discussion of heliocentrism in the *Asclepius* (Corpus Hermeticum II).

including and beyond Giordano Bruno (1548–1600), who promoted an elaborate "mathesis."[6]

Bruno's "mathesis," like the numerologies practiced by Pico, Agrippa, and others before him, was largely influenced by Pythagorean number symbolism combined with forms of cabalistic computation, yet these are not mutually exclusive with the more self-referential system of "mathematics" used in the sciences today—Pythagoras himself developed his timeless geometrical theorems by way of his mystical explorations. Nicolaus Copernicus (1473–1543), who developed the heliocentric theory (model of the solar system) often credited with inaugurating the scientific revolution, referenced Hermes Trismegistus in his work: either the importance given the sun within the Renaissance worldview inspired Copernicus to undertake his calculations or he sought to make his discovery acceptable by legitimizing it with reference to Hermes.[7] Both Robert Fludd (1574–1637), who worked on developing numbered correspondences in mystical diagrams, and Réné Descartes (1596–1650), who developed Cartesian mathematics (including the x-y grid used in calculus), were peers working in the same cultural tradition, although their intellectual adventures ultimately took them in different directions. Johannes Kepler (1571–1630), whose heliocentric laws of planetary motion were key to Newton's later thesis on gravitation, carried out detailed arguments with Robert Fludd, wherein they both referenced the *Corpus Hermeticum* in detail.[8] Later in the same

6   To review these primary sources, see Brian Copenhaver's *The Book of Magic: From Antiquity to Enlightenment* (New York: Penguin Books, 2015), which includes substantial material from Renaissance figures (Pico, Ficino, Agrippa, Dee, Bruno, and more). Here I follow discussions in Yates, *Giordano Bruno*, as well as Frances Yates, *The Art of Memory* (London: Routledge, 1966).

7   Regarding Copernicus and Renaissance mathematics broadly speaking, see Yates, *Giordano Bruno*, 146–56.

8   Regarding Descartes, Kepler, and Fludd, see Yates, *Giordano Bruno*, 432–54.

century, calculus was arguably the *caput mortuum* of Newton's (1642–1726) alchemical search for the Philosopher's Stone (if not the Stone itself), his theory of ether Hermetic cosmogony in the language of science.[9] The conceptual vocabulary of his physics (e.g., "attraction," "repulsion") was adopted from the Hermeticist Jakob Böhme via famous alchemist Henry More.[10]

Of course, the oeuvres of Descartes or Newton result from multiple, contingent historical processes. They cannot be attributed to the Hermetica alone, yet beyond the connections briefly outlined above, the coevolution of Hermetic philosophy with the Classical tradition of the "art of memory" also had much to do with the development of calculus and what came to be known as the "scientific method."

Briefly put, in the Classical periods of Greek and Roman history, the "art of memory" was a method used by rhetoricians: one was to find natural or man-made architecture where there is internal differentiation and associate parts of a speech with mental images to be imprinted on the spaces offered by the architecture. It was understood that words are easier to remember when associated with images, and that the images that are easiest to remember are ones that are wondrous, personify, and involve action or unfamiliar combinations. As Yates recounts, in the Aristotelian tradition the art was merely instrumental (whether chosen images possessed any meaningful

9   *Caput Mortuum* means "dead head" or "worthless remains." In alchemy it denotes a useless substance left over from a chemical operation such as sublimation. Regarding Newton, see, e.g., Klaus Vondung, "Millenarianism, Hermeticism, and the Search for a Universal Science," in *Science, Pseudoscience, and Utopianism in Early Modern Thought*, ed. Stephen McKnight (Columbia, MO: University of Missouri Press, 1992), 138; Richard S. Westfall, "Newton and the Hermetic Tradition," in *Science, Medicine and Society in the Renaissance: Essays in Honor of Walter Pagel*, ed. Allen G. Debus (New York: Science History Publications, 1972).

10 See Ernst Benz, *The Theology of Electricity*, trans. Wolfgang Taraba (Allison Park, PA: Pickwick Publications, 1989).

correspondence to words was irrelevant), yet in the Platonic tradition, mnemonic images should be expressive of the transcendental reality. Throughout the Middle Ages, the art of memory was used largely as a way of remembering (Christian) vices and virtues (spiritual concepts were to be remembered by way of emotion-arousing images), yet in the Renaissance, Hermetic philosophy influenced growing Neoplatonic applications: the art was to provide memory of divine, universal knowledge—just as the Egyptians infused statues with cosmic power, so would Ficino's talismans draw down celestial insights. It was precisely because man is a microcosm, divine in his origin, that in the work of both Fludd and Bruno (and beyond) he may come to "remember" the divine knowledge he contains. Archetypal images exist in a confused chaos, yet properly inspired mnemonic techniques will find their proper order and thus restore to man his full complement of divine powers.[11]

The systematizing impulse of the Classical art of memory thus became associated with memorizing (or channeling) universal truths, and ultimately with *deducing* knowledge. Ramon Lull (1235–1316), who had crafted a system of concentric wheels hosting revolving alphabets (this particular *ars combinandi* primarily influenced by cabalism), had been concerned with the memorization of procedures, first introducing movement into the art, whereas Giordano Bruno (1548–1600) blended the Classical art of memory and Lullism by arranging pictures on rotating concentric wheels instead.[12] For his part, Descartes

---

11 Throughout this passage I follow Paolo Rossi, *Logic and the Art of Memory* (Chicago: University of Chicago Press, 2000), 80, 91–95; Yates, *Art of Memory*. Regarding Classical art during the Middle Ages, see Yates *Art of Memory*, chapters 1–3; regarding Ficino's talismans, see 154–55; regarding the microcosm in Bruno and Fludd, see 217, 339 (Yates discusses both at length throughout the work).

12 Regarding Lull and Bruno, see Rossi, *Logic*, chapter 2 (29–60), 80, 91–95; Yates, *Art of Memory*, 176, 188–90. Cabalist practices developed in Spain in Lull's time included combining the letters of the Hebrew alphabet to form names of God (the Zohar was written at this time);

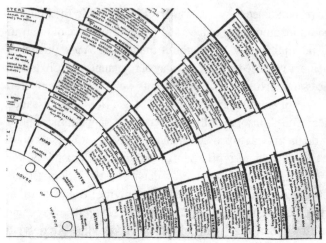

Fig. 1. Sketch of Giulio Camillo's "memory theatre." "[I]f the ancient orators, wishing to place from day to day the parts of speeches which they had to relate, confided them to frail places as frail things, it is right that we, wishing to store up eternally the eternal value of all things which can be expressed in speech . . . should assign them to eternal places" (from Camillo's *L'idea de la Teatro* [1550]).

(1596–1650) proposed that "out of unconnected images should be composed new images common to them all." Outlining his method in a letter in 1619, he proposed to go beyond the *Ars Brevis* of Lull to create a new science that would solve all questions regarding quantity.[13] In the introduction to his encyclopedia, Liebniz (1646–1716) informs us that "here will be found a general science, a new logic, a new method, an *Ars reminiscendi* or Mnemonica, an *Ars Characteristica* or Symbolica, an *Ars Combinatoria* or Lulliana, a Cabala of the Wise, a Magia Naturalis, in short all sciences will be here contained as in an

see Yates, *Art of Memory*, 177, referencing in turn Gershom Scholem, *Major Trends in Jewish Mysticism* (Jerusalem: Schocken Publishing House, 1941).

13 See Yates, *Art of Memory*, 374–75, citing Descartes's *Cogitationes Privatae*. See also this quotation and related discussion in Rossi, *Logic*, 113.

Fig. 2. The *Scala intellectus* (depicting the *Ars Combinatoria*) as it appears in the *Liber de ascendu et descensu intellectus*, Ramon Lull (1512).

Ocean."[14] Ultimately, Liebniz puts numbers where Bruno had put images and thus uses the principles of the *Ars Combinatoria* to develop his calculus.[15]

The principles of order and arrangement of the Classical art thus gradually develop into the logic of classification and increasingly complex forms of algebra. The modern scientific "tree diagram" used for typology is a memory place system, and the letter notations of science are in many ways the "places" of the Classical art.[16] Unified science was inspired by a conception of reality itself as a living unity. The Cartesian plane utilizes vertical and horizontal axes pertaining to different orders, the combination of which indicates semantic syntheses, as was first the case in the memory theatre of Giulio Camillo (1480–1544) (see Fig. 1). Descartes's main innovation was to move from the qualitative to the quantitative use of number: it

---

14   Cited in Yates, *Art of Memory*, 385, referencing Leibniz's *Introductio ad Encyclopaediam arcanam*. See also citation and discussion in Rossi, *Logic*, 191.

15   See Yates, *Art of Memory*, 384. In 1659, Sebastien Izquierdo insisted that the Lullian art be mathematized, substituting numbers for images or letters (see Yates, *Art of Memory*, 379), a move which arguably presaged Liebniz's calculus (see Rossi, *Logic*, chapters 5, 8). Yates provides a full discussion in chapter 17 (regarding Liebniz, see especially *Art of Memory*, 380–84).

16   See Rossi, *Logic*, 42, 114, chapter 5 passim. Regarding "deduction" in the work of Descartes, see Rossi, *Logic*, 124–26; for summary remarks concerning the "art of memory" in the work of Bacon and Descartes, see Rossi, *Logic*, 128. Giambattista Vico's (1668–1744) recrafting of the art of memory also anticipates the modern science of hermeneutics: the Neoplatonist link between imagination and the universe is reposited in the development of human consciousness, i.e., between familiar images of the present and unfamiliar ones of the past; in the words of Patrick H. Hutton, "Hermes . . . taught humankind the art of communication. He did so by travelling from familiar to strange places and back again. Hermes taught humans to understand the unfamiliar by relating it to the familiar." (Students of anthropology might also give pause.) Patrick H. Hutton "The Art of Memory Reconceived: From Rhetoric to Psychoanalysis," *Journal of the History of Ideas* 48, no. 3 (1987): 379.

remains the case that by knowing two (x value and / or y value and / or the relation between them) the third may be found. In short, when transferred to mathematical symbolism, the search for "images for things" resulted in the discovery of new notations that made possible new types of calculation. Most significantly, mathematical notae (images) began to be used for relational concepts, (e.g., dy/dx derivatives).[17]

I offer these abbreviated surveys simply to observe that the "disenchantment" we often hear about in relation to the European Enlightenment is but a tale.[18] During this time "magic" was not in fact disqualified, but rather came to enjoy an increasingly acceptable, even revered, status due to connected advances in mathematics and related practical pursuits. Whereas during the Middle Ages, man's wish to "operate" on the world (as opposed to engaging purely in its contemplation) was attributed to devilish inspiration, within the Hermetic tradition of the Renaissance, man's desire to "operate" on the world was eventually granted as Christian duty. In retrospect, the European historian has enjoyed categorizing certain forms of worldly operation as "magical" and others as "scientific," yet the distinction is anachronistic. Operating with number in the higher sphere of religious magic was continuous with operating with number in the sphere of what Tommaso Campanella

---

17 See Louis Couturat, *La logique de Leibniz: d'apres les documents inédits* (Paris: Félix Alcan, 1901), 84–85; see also Rossi, *Logic*, chapter 8. Following alchemists and astrologers, Liebniz sought characters that represent reality as nearly as possible. Mathematical notae may appear to be farther from reality than images of persons, animals, etc., yet not if we realize that what is now being symbolized is *relationships* (vs. objects); the variable x as a sign does not resemble the signified (indeed, it is meant to signify "any given thing"), yet the equation involving x resembles the action, relationship, or process of change that the annotator wishes to capture.

18 The usage of "disenchantment" to describe the "iron cage of rationality" characterizing the modern West was coined by Max Weber; see, e.g., H.H. Gerth and C. Wright Mills, ed., *From Max Weber: Essays in Sociology* (New York: Routledge, 2009).

called, in reference to the mechanics of pulleys, "real artificial magic."[19] If observers are now inclined to separate out calculus from "magic," it is only because we have defined "magic" in retrospect as activity that is useless, unfounded, and misguided.[20]

At this juncture we do well to begin considering the question of gender in relation to the "public sphere" and worldly operation broadly speaking. After all, as "magic" itself was gaining respect in certain elite quarters, women were being persecuted as witches precisely for practicing "magic," wherein we may observe that the perceived danger was not "magic" itself but the gender of its practitioner. While men's "operation" on the world was sanctioned, women's equivalent "operation" was increasingly targeted as heresy. As Barbara Ehrenreich and Deirdre English first pointed out in their feminist reappraisal of the witch hunts, "witches" were generally no more than lay healers, "wise women," and midwives— indeed, proper empiricists who had "developed an extensive understanding of bones and muscles, herbs and drugs" while those who have gone down in history as the "fathers of science" were still "trying to turn lead into gold." More than a persecution of "magic" broadly put, the witch hunts were a gendered class war wherein elite males forcibly took over both the conceptual and practical realm of healing from peasant women; as the fifteenth-century *Malleus Maleficarum* explains, "If a woman dare to cure without having studied she is a witch and must die."[21]

---

19   See Yates, *Art of Memory*, 147.

20   We thus approach "magic" as a socially constructed category; see, e.g., Stanley Jeyaraja Tambiah, *Magic, Science, Religion, and the Scope of Rationality* (Cambridge: Cambridge University Press, 1990).

21   Barbara Ehrenreich and Deirdre English, *Witches, Midwives and Nurses: A History of Women Healers* (New York: The Feminist Press, 2010 [1973]), 53, 56 (the *Malleus Maleficarum* is quoted on 56). Previous analyses largely failed to consider the witch hunts as consolidation of patriarchal power; see, e.g., Wallace Notestein, *A History of Witchcraft in England from 1558 to 1718* (New York: Thomas

Ehrenreich and English therefore anticipate Silvia Federici's more recently acclaimed work undertaken within the Marxist tradition, which articulates the witch hunt as a phenomenon of "primitive accumulation": just as land, air, and water must first be enclosed as "resources" before the capitalist may profit from the commodities they are then used to produce, so were women enclosed as (reduced to) mere bodies by way of the witch hunts.[22] The persecution of "magic" among "witches" throughout the peasantry was, in fact, a disciplinary measure directed specifically at poor women insofar as it served to enforce the logic of private property, wage work, and the transformation of women into (re)producers of labor. Whereas a common popular misconception of the witch hunts is that they were instigated by peasant men who had not yet discovered "rationality," they were in fact specifically organized by the Church and modernizing European state, wherein many decades of propagandizing were necessary before reliable complicity among peasant men was achieved. Of course, the fear-mongering by authorities that inspired the witch hunts focused obsessively on baby killing, and women's traditional knowledge of birth control ("magic") was indeed being put to good use at the time: the poor dispossessed by the enclosure of the commons could no longer afford to raise children. Fears around a declining population (workforce) and the reproductive autonomy of lower-class women (practicing birth control) was ultimately what distinguished the witch from the Renaissance magician, who demonologists

---

Y. Crowell Company, 1968); H.R. Trevor-Roper, *The European Witch-Craze of the Sixteenth and Seventeenth Centuries* (Harmondsworth: Penguin Books, 1969).

22 See Federici, *Caliban*; regarding the original theorization of "primitive accumulation," see Karl Marx, *Capital*, vol. 1 (London: Penguin Books, 1990 [1867]), chapters 26–33; see especially Ehrenreich and English, *Witches, Midwives and Nurses*, 28–29 to consider the intersection of their analysis with that of Federici.

consistently passed over. In fact, the devilish activities of the "baby-killing" witch were often plagiarized from the High Magical repertoire.[23]

---

23 Federici, *Caliban*; see also Ulinka Rublack, *The Astronomer and the Witch: Johannes Kepler's Fight for His Mother* (Oxford: Oxford University Press, 2015), where we behold one "magical" man given the status of Imperial Mathematician, while his "magical" mother is imprisoned for witchcraft.

Low Dermott. del.

A Scale of ten Cubits.

Plan.

A Scale of ten Cubits: (or 240 Inches) according to Josephus.

Fig. 3. "The Masonic Arch." Practical knowledge of the arch keystone, which effectively redistributes weight, arrived alongside many "ancient" mystical treatises. Such operative knowledge of masonry led to the building of great cathedrals, as well as to the guilds of stonemasons after which Freemasons fashioned themselves. This particular arch image is by Laurence Dermott (1783).

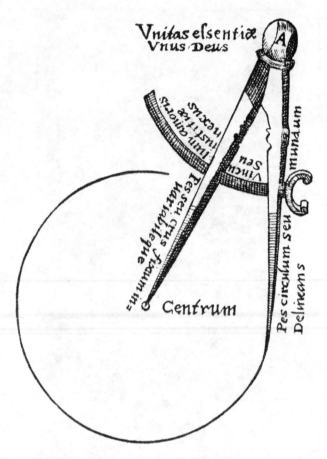

Fig. 4. "The Mystical Compass," Robert Fludd (1617).

Fig. 5. "Figura Mentis" and "Figura Intellectus," Giordano Bruno (1588).

Fig. 6. The compass is again associated with power, here in a certain geometrical and gendered arrangement, by William Blake in "The Ancient of Days," in *Europe: A Prophecy* (1794)—"When he sets a compass upon the face of the deep" (Proverbs 8:27).

Freemasonry, Pantheism, and the Hermetic Tradition

In the hands of power, Hermetic doctrines served to inspire new confidence and justification to assert worldly dominion over all levels of being, yet the same constellation of ideas was also mobilized "from below" to influence the emergent social levelling projects of the modern left. When it became both religious and dignified for "the great miracle of man" to operate on the world, the exertion of existential powers by men with subversive intent was also subjectively validated and socially legitimized. Herein we consider how the Hermetica was fundamental to the emergence of new social movements against systemic power, specifically Freemasonry and the revolutionary brotherhoods that proliferated during the eighteenth and nineteenth centuries.

Unlike the millenarian and heretic movements before them, these more "modern" social movements consisted of literate radicals more so than peasants and were decisively masculine public spheres. Women's power within the peasant and heretic movements was ambiguous and never unchallenged, but women were certainly actively involved, partially because the renovated and syncretic Christian cosmologies crafted during the Crusades granted them new footholds, and partially because women had the most to lose in the privatization of the commons.[1] Freemasonry, on the other hand, is what

---

1   See Silvia Federici, *Caliban and the Witch: Women, the Body and Primitive Accumulation* (New York: Autonomedia, 2004).

social movements look like after the witch hunts: just as alchemists played at the creation of life while arresting feminine control over biological creation, speculative Masonry emerges in which elite males worship the "Grand Architect" upon the ashes of artisans' guilds, while real builders are starving. By the time of the Grand Lodge's establishment in London in 1717, the trade secrets of operative masons had become the spiritual secrets of speculative ones, lodge membership now thoroughly replaced by literate men lured by the ceremony, ritual, and a secret magical history supposedly dating back to the time of King Solomon and the Grand Architect of his temple, Hiram Abiff—Freemasonry itself has always involved a fantastic pastiche of Hermetic and cabalistic lore.[2] (We may also observe a

---

2   Regarding Hermeticist currents in speculative Masonry, see Jean
    Tourniac, *Vie et perspectives de la franc-maçonnerie traditionelle*,
    2nd ed. (Paris: Dervy-Livres, 1978); Regarding the specific links
    Freemasons made between ancient Egypt and Freemasonry, see, e.g.,
    the minutes of Le Conseil de l'Ordre du Grand Orient, April 25, 1887,
    reprinted in Christian Lauzeray, *L'Égypte ancienne et la franc-maçonnerie* (Paris: Éditeur Guy Trédaniel, 1988). J.P. Dubreuil, *Histoire des
    franc-maçons* (Bruxelles: H.I.G. François, 1838) analyzes ritual form,
    dress, ceremonial objects, art, and catechism to illustrate shared
    allegories in the Egyptian, Jewish, and Freemasonic traditions. See
    also Claude-Antoine Thory, *Histoire de la fondation du Grand Orient
    de France* (Paris: l'Imprimerie de Nouzou, 1812). Further references
    in English regarding the social history of Freemasonry include
    Margaret C. Jacob, "Freemasonry and the Utopian Impulse," in
    Millenarianism and Messianism in English Literature and Thought,
    ed. Richard H. Popkin (New York: E.J. Brill, 1988); Margaret Jacob,
    The Radical Enlightenment: Pantheists, Freemasons and Republicans
    (London: George Allen & Unwin, 1981); J.M. Roberts, *The Mythology
    of the Secret Societies* (London: Secker and Warburg, 1972). See also
    the bibliography of primary source materials in Dr. William Wynn
    Westcott, *A Catalogue Raisonné of Works on the Occult Sciences, vol. 3:
    Freemasonry, a Catalogue of Lodge Histories (England), with a Preface*
    (London: F.L. Gardner, 1912). Note there are significant differences
    between the social development and organization of Freemasonry
    in England and on the European continent, yet as their consideration is not entirely crucial to our present study these will be bracketed here.

possible influence of the Classical art of memory within the Freemasonic penchant for columns and arches in its symbolism, as well as in its reverence for the "Divine Architect.")[3]

One Hermetic aspect of the Masonic cosmology that is key for our discussion, addressed below, is the notion that man and society tend toward perfection. Here the work of Spinoza (1632–1677) was also, together and separately, an inspiration in this regard. In his "Theological-Political Treatise" (1670), Spinoza arguably provides the founding text of modern liberalism by effectively conflating the "chosen people" and the chosen "state" or "society," and by relativizing the gift of prophecy as an imaginative (vs. rational) capacity of men and women of all traditions ("gentiles").[4] The import of Spinoza's complete oeuvre, across time and audience, is of course diverse and contested, yet it is clear that with the "Treatise," which was persecuted time and again as heresy, he equipped contemporary European radicals with a dynamic philosophy that unified, divinized, and animated the universe, as well as honoring a deterministic vision of man and nature, thus providing a new religious vision and a renovated foundation for social resistance at once.[5]

Contemporaries came to term this orientation "pantheism." This word, apparently first used by John Toland (1670–1722), was taken up during the period in question to refer to a

---

3   See Yates, *Art of Memory*, 304.

4   See Benedict de Spinoza, *Theological-Political Treatise*, ed. Jonathan Israel, (Cambridge: Cambridge University Press, 2007 [1670]), especially chapter 2, "On the Prophets," [1], [3]; chapter 3, "On the Vocation of the Hebrews," [8], [9], passim.

5   See also, e.g., Benedict de Spinoza, *Ethics* (New York: Oxford University Press, 2000). Regarding the charges of Spinoza's work within the culture of the "radical Enlightenment," see Jonathan Israel, *Radical Enlightenment* (Oxford: Oxford University Press, 2001); Jonathan Israel, *A Revolution of Mind: Radical Enlightenment and the Intellectual Origins of Modern Democracy* (Princeton, NJ: Princeton University Press, 2010); see also Jacob, *The Radical Enlightenment*, regarding articulations of "pantheism" and their relation to Spinoza's ideas.

metaphysics that reemphasized the vitalistic "spirit in matter" qualities of nature and tended to deify the material order in the process.[6] A new faith in scientific progress therefore encouraged the conception of temporal institutions both as permanent and as vehicles for enacting fantasies of social progress: a new heaven on earth would be manifest through the works of men themselves.

Precise lines of logical or historical causality between the work of Spinoza and that of Giordano Bruno, the development of Freemasonry, and the Rosicrucian manifestos, to name but a few contemporaneous cultural elements of the seventeenth century, are not to be drawn clearly, yet their complementary sensibility is clear. We know that the first recorded Freemasons were Robert Moray (initiated in 1641) and Elias Ashmole (initiated in 1646). We can be fairly confident that the aspirations to universal reform found in the pseudonymous seventeenth-century Rosicrucian manifestos owe something to the popular ("cult") interest in the ideas of Hermeticists Giordano Bruno and Tommaso Campanella, and that all of these appear to have been imported into English popular culture by Robert Fludd, possibly encouraging those inspired to seek religious, scientific, and social reform in the name of universal progress by forming societies of like-minded peers, which may include the institution of Freemasonry.[7] What is of particular interest

---

6   See, e.g., Jacob, *The Radical Enlightenment*, xi, 32–33.

7   See Frances Yates, *The Rosicrucian Enlightenment* (London: Routledge, 1972), chapter 15 for discussion and further sources regarding the relationship of Freemasonry and Rosicrucianism; briefly presented as well in Yates, *Giordano Bruno*, 414–16. Note that Yates critically follows Paul Arnold, *Histoire des Rose-Croix et les origines de la franc-maçonnerie* (Paris: Mercure de France, 1955). See also Antoine Faivre, *Theosophy, Imagination, Tradition: Studies in Western Esotericism*, trans. Christine Rhone (New York: State University of New York Press, 2000); Raffaella Faggionato, *A Rosicrucian Utopia in Eighteenth Century Russia: The Masonic Circle of N.I. Novikov* (Netherlands: Springer, 2005).

to our discussion is that Freemasonic society was decidedly anticlerical, yet espoused a pantheism that infused its social levelling project with sacred purpose.

The *Traité des Trois Imposteurs* that Masons circulated clandestinely during the eighteenth century refers to Moses, Jesus, and Mohammed as the three "Imposters" in question, yet the coterie who printed it included Toland, who in his *Pantheisticon* (1720) elaborated a new ritual that claimed to combine the traditions of Druids and ancient Egyptians and included the following call and response: "Keep off the prophane People / *The Coast is clear, the Doors are shut, all's safe*/ All things in the world are one, And one in All in all things / *What's all in All Things is God, Eternal and Immense* / Let us sing a Hymn Upon the Nature of the Universe." Masons imagined themselves simultaneously the creators of a new egalitarian social order and the protagonists of cosmic regeneration, all articulated in the language of sacred architecture. Theirs was a pyramidal initiatic society of rising degrees and reserved secrets, but one in which all men met "upon the level."[8]

The Masonic levelling project was not altogether radical. It is true that Masonic lodges were frequented by elite men who instrumentalized them to further consolidate their power, and that the Masonic project was one of limited reforms, one to which Jews, women, servants, and manual laborers were

---

8   See Jacob, "Freemasonry and the Utopian Impulse," 127–30; regarding the *Traité des Trois Imposteurs*, see Jacob, *The Radical Enlightenment*, chapter 7; the quotation from the *Pantheisticon* is on 122–23; see also xiii. See also Roberts, *The Mythology of the Secret Societies*, chapter 2.

Song II in the *Universal Masonic Library* (1855)
Ere God the universe began
In one rude chaos matter lay
And wild disorder overran
Nor knew of light one glimmering ray.
While in darkness o'er the whole
Confusion reign'd without control

Then God arose, his thunders hurl'd
And bade the elements arise
In air he hung the pendent world
And o'er it spread the azure skies.
Stars in circles caus'd to run
And in the centre fix'd the sun.

Then man he call'd forth out of dust
And form'd him with a having soul
All things committed to his trust
And made him ruler of the whole
But, ungrateful unto Heaven
The rebel was from Eden driven.

From thence proceeded all our woes
Nor could mankind one comfort cheer
Until Freemasonry arose
And form'd another Eden here:
'Tis only on Masonic ground
Pleasure with innocence is found.

'Tis here the purest fountains flow
Here nought corrupt can enter in
Here trees of knowledge stately grow
Whose fruit we taste, exempt from sin
In friendship sweet we still abound
While guardian angels hover round.

Fig. 7. Song found in William Preston, *The Universal Masonic Library, vol. 3: Preston's Illustrations of Masonry*, (New York: W. Leonard & Co., African Masonic Agency, 1855), 364–65. This work begins with a section titled "Reflections on the Symmetry and Proportion in the Works of Nature and on the Harmony and Affection among the Various Species of Beings." With respect to the song reprinted here, it is explained that "the following Anthems, Glees were performed at the Union," and the song is forwarded with the information "Tune, Rule, Britannia."

denied entry.[9] It is also true that the Masonic ideal of merit as the only fair distinction allowed room to critique the tension between formal ideals and actual practice, and that Masonic lodges were the first formal public association in eighteenth-century Britain to take up the cause of the "workers' question"—albeit on a purely philanthropic level—by founding hospices, schools, and assistance centers for proletarian workers.[10] In prerevolutionary France, lodges first began accepting small artisans, then proletarian workers as well, lowering fees and abolishing the literacy requirement for entrance to this end. By 1789, there were between twenty thousand and fifty thousand members in over six hundred lodges, and it was no longer possible for participants to reasonably claim they were manifesting an egalitarian social order by merely gathering

---

9   See, e.g., Alberto Valín Fernández, "De masones y revolucionarios: una reflexión en torno de este encuentro," *Anuario Brigantino* 28 (2005): 173–98, as well as his monograph length work, Alberto Valín Fernández, *Masonería y revolución: del mito literario a la realidad historica* (Santa Cruz de Tenerife: Ediciones Idea, 2008). In the words of one Bordeaux lodge master (1745), "le privilege de l'Égalité deviendroit [sic] un abus bien dangereux, si sous ce prétexte on admettrait indifferément tous les états" [The privilege of equality would become a very dangerous abuse if on this pretext we were to admit members of all classes (états) without distinction], cited in Roberts, *The Mythology of the Secret Societies*, 50, who is citing William Doyle, *The Parlementaires of Bordeaux at the End of the Eighteenth Century 1775–1790* (PhD diss., Oxford University, 1967), 338. According to another contemporary Freemason (1744), the sister lodges organized for women were but for "immoral purposes" and "beguiling" women "into thinking they had penetrated the secrets," in Roberts, *The Mythology of the Secret Societies*, 50–51, citing *La Franc-maçonne ou révélation des mystères des franc-maçons* (Brussels: 1744), 11–15.

10 See Jacob, "Freemasonry and the Utopian Impulse," especially 142; Valín Fernández, "De masones y revolucionarios," 182, discusses Freemasonic philanthropy related to the "workers' question."

to discuss literature, science, and the cultivation of Masonic wisdom.[11]

---

11 Regarding reforms in favor of proletarian entry, see Valín Fernández, "De masones y revolucionarios," 183, who follows the work of André Combes, *Les trois siècles de la franc-maçonnerie française* (Paris: Dervy, 2006). The figures given regarding lodge membership in 1789 are from Daniel Mornet, *Les origines intellectuelles de la Révolution française* (Paris: Librairie Armand Colin, 1933), and Daniel Ligou, "La franc-maçonnerie française au XVIII siècle (positions des problèmes et état des questions)," *Information Historique* (1964). For an overview in English, see Margaret C. Jacob, *Strangers Nowhere in the World: The Rise of Cosmopolitanism in Early Modern Europe* (Philadelphia: University of Pennsylvania Press, 2006). With respect to Masonic reform and the "workers' question" in Spain, see Ángeles González Fernández, "Masonería y modernización social: transformación del obrero en ciudadano 1868–1931," *Bulletin d'histoire contemporaine de l'Espagne* 32, no. 36 (2003), 89–116; José Antonio Ferrer Benimeli, "La masonería española y la cuestion social," *Estudios de Historia Social* 40, no. 1 (1987): 7–47.

The Revolutionary Brotherhoods

Here we arrive at the question of "conspiratorial" revolutionary brotherhoods that has been exploited in paranoid intrigue. On one hand, due to the utopian rhetoric developed in the Masonic "public" sphere, some members became directly involved in revolutionary activities, both in France before the Revolution, as well as throughout Europe in the years immediately following. On the other hand, it is true that many revolutionaries who were not necessarily Masons made use of the lodges' existing infrastructure and social networks to further their cause. Yet others simply adopted Masonic iconography and organizational style, which had accrued a measure of symbolic power and legitimacy, in developing their own revolutionary associations. It is not possible in retrospect to distinguish entirely between these phenomena, the salient point being that the revolutionary brotherhoods that proliferated at the turn of the nineteenth century derived much of their power from their association with perennial secrets and magical power, and that this imaginary and their related style of social organization were fundamental to the development of what we come to recognize as modern revolutionism.[1]

---

1   I proceed to summarize below, yet a detailed genealogy of the brotherhoods in question can be found in Julius Braunthal, *History of the International, vol. 1, 1864–1914* (New York: Frederick A. Praeger Publishers, 1967), chapters 4–6. Eric Hobsbawm, *Primitive Rebels: Studies in Archaic Forms of Social Movement in the 19th and 20th Centuries* (New York: W.W. Norton & Co., 1959), although inflected

Adam Weishaupt (1748–1830), a young Bavarian professor who founded the Illuminati in 1776, was one of few convinced egalitarians of his day. His revolutionary agenda involved the complete dismantling of the state, the Church, and the institution of private property, all justified by a revamped Christian millenarianism affected by readings of Jean-Jacques Rousseau and the Eleusinian mysteries and organizationally inspired by the secret association of the Pythagoreans.[2] According to Weishaupt, our true "fall from grace" was our submission to the rule of government:

> Let us take Liberty and Equality as the great aim of [Christ's] doctrines and Morality as the way to attain it, and everything in the New Testament will be comprehensible.... Man is fallen from the condition of Liberty and Equality, the *state of prenature*. He is under subordination and civil bondage, arising from the vices of man. This is the *fall*, and *original sin*. The *kingdom of grace* is that restoration which may be brought about by Illumination.[3]

---

with a critical Marxist bias, provides another overview in English. J.M. Roberts, *The Mythology of the Secret Societies* (London: Secker and Warburg, 1972), chapter 7, discusses the "seedtime of the political secret societies."

2   See René Le Forestier, *Les Illuminés de Bavière et la franc-maçonnerie allemande* (Genève: Slatkine Megariotis Reprints, 1974 [1914]) or Jonathan Israel, *A Revolution of Mind: Radical Enlightenment and the Intellectual Origins of Modern Democracy* (Princeton, NJ: Princeton University Press, 2010) (they both cite further sources in German); Roberts, *The Mythology of the Secret Societies*, refers to Le Forestier.

3   Weishaupt in a communiqué titled "Spartacus to Cato" (Spartacus was Weishaupt's pseudonym), in John Robison, *Proofs of a Conspiracy against All the Religions and Governments of Europe, Carried on in the Secret Meetings of Freemasons, Illuminati, and Reading Societies* (Dublin: W. Watson and Son, 1798), 92–93. To consult Weishaupt in his original German, see "Spartacus to Cato" (March 5, 1778) in Richard van Dülman, *Der Geheimbund der Illuminaten* (Stuttgart: Frommann-Holzboog Verlag, 1975), 220.

Yet, "Do you really believe it would be useful," he asked, "as long as countless barriers still remain, to preach to men a purified religion, a superior philosophy, and the art of self-government? . . . Should not all these organizational vices and social ills be corrected gradually and quietly before we may hope to bring about this golden age, and wouldn't it be better, in the meanwhile, to propagate the truth by way of secret societies? Do we not find traces of the same secret doctrine in the most ancient schools of wisdom?"[4] For Weishaupt, only the "immanent revolution of the human spirit" (*die bevorstehende Revolution des menschlichen Geistes*), driven by a "widely propagated universal Enlightenment" (*verbreitete allgemeine Aufklärung*) will break the chains of tyranny, but repressive political conditions required a discreet Enlightened revolutionary elite in the meantime.[5]

Weishaupt had joined a Masonic lodge in 1774 but had left shortly after, not satisfied with the level of critique he found therein. A year after founding his more radical group, however, the members together decided in 1777 to join lodges once more in order to find new recruits, and the strategy worked. The Illuminati grew from Weishaupt and five students in 1776 to fifty-four members in five Bavarian cities by 1779, and eventually extended to Italy, Lyon, and Strasbourg to include figures such as Goethe, Schiller, Mozart, and Herder. The pyramid structure of the network, modelled on Masonic form, was organized into three grades (the Minervale, Minervale Illuminato, and inner circle of Areopagites) and became both an agency for the transmission of commonplace

---

4   Le Forestier's French translation of the full passage from German may be found in Le Forestier, *Les Illuminés de Bavière et la franc-maçonnerie allemande*, 28; the English translation above (from the French) is my own.
5   See Israel, *A Revolution of Mind*, 78; Israel cites Adam Weishaupt, "Anrede an die neu aufzunehmenden Illuminatos dirigentes," found in van Dülman, *Der Geheimbund der Illuminaten*.

Enlightenment ideas and a "quasi-religious sect" in which men met to contemplate the utopian regeneration of society.[6] Its growth was short-lived however. In 1783, a Minervale Illuminato left the order discontented and shared its radical ideas with his employer, a duchess of the Bavarian royal family. Ensuing suspicions that the Illuminati were connected with an Austrian plot to annex the electorate (and perhaps worse) alarmed the government and a repressive campaign began.

The character of the ensuing persecution is well summarized by Jonathan Israel, who discusses the agitation of contemporary observers, including the ultrareactionary court official Ludwig Adolf Christian von Grolman (1749–1809), who published a collection of German Illuminatist documents, *Die neuesten Arbeiten des Spartacus und Philo*, in 1793. This court official protested that the highest grades of the order were, in effect, "a clandestine vehicle for the propagation of materialist and atheistic ideas and that at the core of the highest mysteries of the organization's first grade, the so-called *Philosophengrad* (philosopher's grade), lay unadulterated *Spinozismus* (Spinozism)," which is to say that "everything that exists is matter, that God and the universe are the same, and that all organized religion is a political deception devised by ambitious men."[7] By the end of the eighteenth century stories vilifying the Illuminati and the Freemasons—who were all "under its control"—were in full force. Fearing the death penalty, members went into hiding or exile.

---

6   See Roberts, *Mythology of the Secret Societies*, 118–24 (the direct quote is from 122); Israel, *A Revolution of Mind*, 73–80.

7   See Israel, *A Revolution of Mind*, 74, citing in turn Martin Mulsow, "Adam Weishaupt als Philosoph," and Wolfgang Riedel, "Aufklärung und Macht: Schiller, Abel und die *Illuminaten*," in *Die Weimarer Klassik und ihre Geheimbünde*, ed. Walter Müller-Seidel and Wolfgang Riedel (Würzburg: Königshausen & Neumann, 2003). For overview in English, see Roberts, *Mythology of the Secret Societies*, 125–28.

The turn of the century saw a proliferation of other revolutionary societies across Europe that mimicked the forms of Freemasonry and the Illuminati, including the Charbonnerie and Carbonari, the Mazzinians and le Monde, all constituting an international network of revolutionary movements that had certain ideological, if not organizational, solidity. The politics of Babeuf (1760–1797), who was imprisoned in the aftermath of the French Revolution as the prime agent of the "The Conspiracy of Equals," and the politics of Philippe Buonarotti (1761–1837), who founded the Sublime Perfect Masters in 1809, likewise bear a family resemblance. We may also note that Babeuf anticipated Proudhon's argument that "property is theft" by forty-three years, explaining during his trial defense that the "institution of private property must necessarily bring about the existence of the fortunate and unfortunate of masters and slaves. The law of *heredity* is supremely abusive … possession by a few is usurpation … whatever an individual hoards of the land and its fruits beyond what he needs for his own nourishment has been stolen from society."[8] Buonarrotti was clearly inspired by Babeuf, as he wrote an entire book about him, discussed below. Buonarotti had a low opinion of established Freemasonry, but nevertheless admitted only Masons into his brotherhood for the express purpose of using established lodges as a nursery for revolutionary ideas in a Christian language. Every candidate for supreme command of the Sublime Perfect Masters had to infiltrate a masonic lodge and rise through its hierarchy to a key position, successfully altering the structure of lodges in Tuscany, Piedmont, and Lombardy by adding a third grade that dovetailed the lodges' hierarchy with their own. Louis August Blanqui (1805–1881) shifted from espousing republicanism to radical democracy

---

8   See Albert Fried and Ronald Sanders, *Socialist Thought: A Documentary History* (New York: Anchor Books, 1964); the quote from Babeuf's trial is found on 63–64.

under Buonarotti's influence, and later created his very own sect—the Society of the Seasons.[9]

It did make certain practical sense to organize in a clandestine fashion, as proposed by both Babeuf and Buonarotti (beyond Weishaupt) at the turn of the century, as following the French Revolution the feudal dynasties of Russia, Austria, Prussia, Italy, and Spain, along with powerful allies in all other European countries and the Catholic Church, had formed their own international organization, pledging themselves to cooperative repressive action within any state where absolute sovereigns felt threatened by, in the words of Tsar Nicholas, "revolutionary inroads."[10] These conservative governmental powers formalized themselves as the "Holy Alliance" at the Congress of Vienna in 1814, and proceeded to cooperate in international publication bans, as well as transnational surveillance and repression of militants. This clearly posed serious practical problems for social revolutionaries. To suggest the prevailing political mood, consider the Fraternal Democrats' reply to the Brussels Democrats (then led by Karl Marx) in 1846: "[Marx] will tell you with what enthusiasm we welcomed his appearance and the reading of your address. . . . We recommend the

---

9   See R.B. Rose, *Gracchus Babeuf: The First Revolutionary Communist* (Stanford: Stanford University Press, 1978); Fried and Sanders, *Socialist Thought*; Elizabeth L. Eisenstein, *The First Professional Revolutionist: Filippo Michele Buonarotti (1761–1837)* (Cambridge, MA: Harvard University Press, 1959), 45, passim. For discussion of Blanqui's influence on Marx, see Braunthal, *History of the International*, 46–52. Regarding the relationship of the Illuminati, Freemasonry, and Carbonari with respect to Italy's *Risorgimento*, see Carlo Francovich, "Gli Illuminati di Weishaupt e l'idea egualitaria in alcune società segrete del Risorgimento," *Movimento Operaio* 4, no. 4 (1952): 553–97. To consider how the international "secret societies" of this time developed and functioned according to local needs and cultural context, see, e.g., P. Savigear, "Some Reflections on Corsican Secret Societies in the Early Nineteenth Century," *International Review of Social History* 19, no. 1 (1974).

10   Cited in Braunthal, *History of the International*, 39.

formation of a democratic congress of all nations, and we are happy to hear that you have publicly made the same proposal. The conspiracy of kings must be answered with the conspiracy of the peoples."[11]

It is worth noting that Marx had read Buonarotti's book *Babeuf and the Conspiracy for Equality*, which conveyed to posterity the ideas of the Babeuvists, including both the need for revolutionary conspiracy and the destruction of private property. Buonarotti's book on the topic first appeared in Brussels in 1828, then two years later in Paris, being translated into English in 1838 by the Chartist leader James Bronterre O'Brien. Marx read the book in 1844 and, together with Engels, sought to arrange a German edition translated by Moses Hess. It is during this time that we see the emergence of the Corresponding Society, the League of the Just, the Communist League, and the Fraternal Democrats mentioned above.[12]

To recapitulate, then, the pyramidal structure of the nineteenth-century revolutionary organizations, in which each level of the pyramid would know only its immediate superiors, clearly had a practical function insofar as it protected revolutionaries from repression in this era of increasingly consolidated international state power and surveillance. The resemblances among groups were not necessarily due to ex-Illuminati members starting up new groups, but rather partially due to the fearful accounts of the Illuminati propagated by governments at the time, which had the ironic effect of inspiring others to try the strategy, as well as due to

11 Cited in Franz Mehring, *Karl Marx: The Story of His Life*, trans. Edward Fitzgerald (London: Allen & Unwin, 1936), 142–43. Regarding the Holy Alliance, see Braunthal, *History of the International*, chapter 5, "The Counterrevolutionary International," especially 37–43.

12 See Braunthal, *History of the International*, 35–36. See also Arthur Lehning, *From Buonarroti to Bakunin: Studies in International Socialism* (Leiden: Brill, 1970). Hobsbawm discusses Marx's developing dissatisfaction with the initiatic society as a revolutionary method in *Primitive Rebels*.

general cultural diffusion, including via Buonarotti's book.[13] The specific organization and ritualization of all this revolutionary activity clearly had other functions as well: the brotherhoods affirmed and unified the aspirations of illuminated men whose purpose it was to steer mankind toward achieving perfection on (this) earth. Bakunin, 32nd degree Mason himself, appeared to feel the same calling when he founded his own secret "International Brotherhood" in Florence in 1864, which mirrored Weishaupt's vision almost exactly one hundred years later.[14] The main difference between the two was that Bakunin's Brotherhood was meant to infiltrate the First International and wrest it from the authoritarian socialists' control, as opposed to infiltrating Masonic lodges in order to wrest them from liberals' control. This is far from the only way in which Masonry and the International Workingman's Association (IWA) coincide.

---

13 John Robison, *Proofs of a Conspiracy*, may be referred to as a primary source document exemplary of a fearful (and perhaps inspirational) account published by contemporary elites. In contrast, see Jean Joseph Mounier, *On the Influence Attributed to Philosophers, Free-Masons, and to the Illuminati on the Revolution of France* (New York: Scholars Facsimiles and Reprints, 1974 [1801]); Mounier responds in part to Robison, who had accused Mounier himself of being part of the conspiracy. See also commentary by Charles William Heckethorn, *The Secret Societies of All Ages and Countries* (London: Richard Bentley and Son, 1875), who argues that Robison attributes disproportionate influence to the Illuminati.

14 Bakunin became a member of the order during the 1840s in Paris; see Nunzio Pernicone, *Italian Anarchism, 1864–1892* (Princeton, NJ: Princeton University Press, 1993), 16, passim, for discussion of both Bakunin's Masonry and his activities in Florence. For an annotated list of anarchist and socialist militants who were Freemasons and a discussion of Freemasonry in relation to the *Commune de Paris*, see Leo Campion, *Le drapeau noir, l'équerre et le compas* (Marseille: Editions Culture et Liberté, 1969).

Illuminism in the IWA

By the mid-nineteenth century many members of Masonic society had come to feel the proletarian struggle coincided with their greater cause, and the use of Masonic organizations as a cover for revolutionary activity was by then a long tradition, as was the tendency to use Masonic rites, customs, and icons to emblematically symbolize the values of equality, solidarity, fraternity, and work.[1] Pierre-Joseph Proudhon, a Mason who lived to see the formation of the International Workingman's Association (IWA), wrote that "The Masonic God is neither Substance, Cause, Soul, Monad, Creator, Father, Logos, Love, Paraclete, Redeemer. . . . God is the personification of universal equilibrium."[2] In Proudhon's day, the British lodges were

---

1   See Alberto Valín Fernández, "De masones y revolucionarios: una reflexión en torno de este encuentro," *Anuario Brigantino* 28 (2005): 181.

2   From *Of Justice in the Revolution and the Church* (1858), cited in Heleno Saña, *El anarquismo, de Proudhon a Cohn-Bendit* (Madrid: Indice, 1970), 40. It is telling of bias that many English reprints of Proudhon do not include such material; for example, Stewart Edwards and Elizabeth Fraser, ed., *Selected Writings of Pierre-Joseph Proudhon* (London: Macmillan, 1969) excludes such excerpts, preferring Proudhon in the following mode: "God is stupidity and cowardice; god is hypocrisy and falsehood; god is tyranny and poverty" (1846). For further discussion and references regarding the religiosity of figures such as Proudhon and Kropotkin, see Harold Barclay, "Anarchist Confrontations with Religion," in *New Perspectives on Anarchism* (Lanham: Lexington Books, 2010) (note the relationship is one of "confrontation"), as well as the synthetic overview and

admitting increasing numbers of proletarian members—
particularly skilled and literate workers—and had come to
support the workers' struggle to the extent that the first pre-
paratory meeting of the IWA on the August 5, 1862, attended by
Karl Marx among others, was held in the Free Masons Tavern.[3]
Many of those in attendance were "socialist Freemasons," a
phrase applied at the time to the members of the small lodges
founded in 1850 and 1858 in London by exiled French republicans, and which involved many members of diverse national
backgrounds—these were named "Memphite" lodges, after
the sacred Egyptian burial ground. The immediate objectives
of the Memphite program were twofold: the struggle against
ignorance through education and helping the proletarians
in their struggle for emancipation by way of Proudhonian
mutual aid associations. Louis Blanc was among the members
of the Memphite lodges (the Loge des Philadelphes), along with
at least seven other founders of the IWA. In Geneva, also, the
local wing of the IWA was often called the Temple Unique and
met in the Masonic lodge of the same name.[4] Many present at
the time observed that the incipient IWA's organizing power
was so weak that if it were not for the organizing efforts of
socialist Freemasons, the official founding meeting of the IWA
on September 28, 1864 would never have come to pass.[5]

Communist and anarchist symbolism, such as the red star
and the circle-A, date back to this period and also have Masonic
origins. The star, which hosts an endless charge of esoteric

---

multiple further sources offered in Alexandre Christoyannopoulos
and Lara Apps, "Anarchism and Religion," in *The Palgrave Handbook
of Anarchism*, ed. Carl Levy and Matthew S. Adams (Basingstoke, UK:
Palgrave Macmillan, 2019).

3   See, e.g., Valín Fernández, "De masones y revolucionarios," 182.
4   See Valín Fernández, "De masones y revolucionarios," 179, 182–84.
5   See Valín Fernández, "De masones y revolucionarios," 182–83. See
    also his main source in this regard, Max Nettlau, *La anarquía a
    través de los tiempos* (Barcelona: Editorial Antalbe, 1979 [1929]), who
    references accounts written by those present at the time.

Fig. 8 The seal of the *Consejo Federal de España de la A.I.T.* (circa 1870).

meanings in both the Hermetic and Pythagorean traditions, had been adopted in the eighteenth century (some say seventeenth) by Freemasons to symbolize the second degree of membership in their association—that of Comrade (*Compañero* and *Camarade* in my sources). Among socialists, it was first used by members of the Memphite lodges and then the IWA. Regarding the circle-A, early versions like the nineteenth-century logo of the Spanish locale of the IWA are clearly composed of the compass, level, and plumb line of Masonic iconography, the only innovation being that the compass and level are arranged to form the letter A inside of a circle.[6]

Over time these symbols have developed a new complement of meanings—many twenty-first-century anarchists don't even know that the star used by communists, anarchists, and Zapatistas alike is the pagan pentagram. They are not reminded of the mathematical perfection of cosmogony when they behold it, or of Giordano Bruno's geometric arts of memory, nor do they necessarily realize there is a genealogical link between the (neo)pagan May Day celebration and today's anarchist May Day marches. Nowadays the May Day march is taken to commemorate the Haymarket massacre (1886), yet it is no coincidence that there was much upheaval in Chicago that day, because revolutionaries had been honoring May Day since before the time of the Illuminati, which was also founded on this symbolic day. In the nineteenth century, these symbolic

---

6   See Valín Fernández, "De masones y revolucionarios," 180–88.

associations were well known by those involved, however, and their adoption reflected how much they resonated with mystical and historical weight. Even Bakunin, while he rejected the personal God of his Russian Orthodox childhood, put forward a pantheistic revolutionism. In a letter to his sister (1836), he wrote, "Let religion become the basis and reality of your life and your actions, but let it be the pure and single-minded religion of divine reason and divine love.... [I]f religion and an inner life appear in us, then we become conscious of our strength, for we feel that God is within us, that same God who creates a new world, a world of absolute freedom and absolute love ... that is our aim."[7]

Bakunin is much better known among anarchists living today for his reversal of Voltaire's famous aphorism—"If God really existed, it would be necessary to abolish him."[8] Throughout the nineteenth century, however, the only people involved in the revolutionary scene who were consistently annoyed by this sort of mysticism were Marx and Engels. Proudhon's ramblings about God as Universal Equilibrium were the sort of thing Marx and Engels objected to and contrasted with their own brand of "scientific socialism"—"the French reject philosophy and perpetuate religion by dragging it over with themselves into the projected new state of society."[9] Bakunin and Marx differed on this point and a number of others, the most famous being the role of the state. Whereas Marx considered a state dictatorship of the proletariat to be a necessary moment in his historical dialectic, Bakunin espoused the notion of a secret revolutionary organi-

---

7   Cited in Arthur Lehning, ed., *Michael Bakunin: Selected Writings* (London, Jonathan Cape Ltd., 1973), 34–35.

8   See Michael Bakunin, *God and the State*, ed. Paul Avrich (New York: Dover Publications Inc., 1970).

9   See Friedrich Engels, "Progress of Social Reform on the Continent," in *Karl Marx and Friedrich Engels: Collected Works*, vol. 3, ed. Robert C. Tucker (New York: International Publishers, 1975), 407.

zation that would "help the people toward self-determination, without the least interference from any sort of domination, even if it be temporary or transitional."[10] Bakunin also wrote that he saw our "only salvation in a revolutionary anarchy directed by a secret collective force"—the only sort of power that he would accept—"because it is the only one compatible with the spontaneity and the energy of the revolutionary movement"; "We must direct the people as invisible pilots, not by means of any visible power, but rather through a dictatorship without ostentation, without titles, without official right, which in not having the appearance of power will therefore be more powerful."[11]

The "dictatorial power" of this secret organization only represents a paradox if we do not recognize the long tradition and larger cosmology within which Bakunin is working. Revolution may be "immanent" in the people, but the guidance of illuminated men working in the "occult" was necessary to guide them in the right direction. Members of his International Brotherhood were to act "as lightning rods to electrify them with the current of revolution" precisely to ensure "that this movement and this organization should never be able to constitute any authorities."[12]

10   Cited in Lehning, *Michael Bakunin*, 191–92.
11   Bakunin cited in Saña, *El anarquismo*, 106.
12   Bakunin cited in Robert M. Cutler, ed., *Mikhail Bakunin: From Out of the Dustbin: Bakunin's Basic Writings, 1869–71* (Ann Arbor, MI: Ardis, 1985).

Theosophy and Other Esoterica
of Nineteenth-Century Socialism

Beyond Bakunin, Robert Owen (1771–1858), Charles Fourier
(1772–1837), and Saint-Simon (1760–1825) are also often cited
as forefathers in standard histories of anarchism.[1] The
Owenites were distinctly anticlerical, attacking all forms of
"religion," but Owen himself was a spiritualist in admiration
of Emmanuel Swedenborg (1688–1772), who taught the arrival
of an "internal millennium." The first Owenite communes
in America were based largely on Swedenborg's teachings.[2]
Charles Fourier, for his part, based his political project on what
he called the Law of Passional Attraction—a series of correspondences in nature that maintain harmony in the universe
and could be applied to human society.[3] Saint-Simonians
aimed at reforming existing institutions, but Fourierists and
Owenites rejected the existing system altogether. Rather than
a mere "changing of the guard," they advocated the creation of

---

1   See, e.g., Peter Marshall, *Demanding the Impossible: A History
    of Anarchism* (London: Fontana Press, 1993); Atindranath Bose, *A
    History of Anarchism* (Calcutta: World Press, 1967); George Woodcock,
    Anarchism: A History of Libertarian Ideas and Movements (Cleveland:
    The World Publishing Co., 1962).

2   See, e.g., Alfred J. Gabay, *The Covert Enlightenment: Eighteenth-
    Century Counterculture and Its Aftermath* (West Chester, PA:
    Swedenborg Foundation Publishers, 2005), xiv, 153–54; Frank E.
    Manuel and Fritzie P. Manuel, *Utopian Thought in the Western World*
    (Cambridge, MA: Harvard University Press, 1979), 585.

3   See Manuel and Manuel, *Utopian Thought in the Western World*,
    chapter 27.

new forms of independent organization within the existing system; hence their "precursor" status to anarchism, perennially defined by the notion of building a new world within the shell of the old, whether via "networks," communes, or syndicates, as well as by a rejection of state power.

Meanwhile, Darwin's treatise on evolution lent itself to theories of social change that dovetailed with revolutionary thought—a distinction between *evolution* and *revolution* in nineteenth-century utopian socialism would be rather forced. The insight that the natural world was characterized by evolving beings blended easily with the concept of cosmic regeneration—adaptive "process" became "progress," a tendency toward perfection. Indeed, many contemporary thinkers extended the idea from plants and animals to human society, the most famous version of such a move being "Social Darwinism," traceable to Herbert Spencer, the actual author of the phrase "survival of the fittest."[4] Here Darwin is recuperated within the transcendentalist tradition to lend weight to the Hobbesian conception of the state of nature—the "war of each against all" so convenient to capitalist ideology. Anarchist natural philosophers of the nineteenth century read Darwin differently. Anarchist patriarch Peter Kropotkin posited "mutual aid" as a prime "factor of evolution" (1914), which we ourselves may manifest as we lead civilization toward egalitarian harmony.[5] It is also worth noting that Kropotkin's key contribution to anarchist theory was heavily influenced by Mechnikov, who was in turn inspired by a long stint in revolutionary Japan, and who had written of the world being divided into three spheres— inorganic, biological, and sociological—each governed by its

---

4   See Charles Darwin, *On the Origin of Species: A Facsimile of the First Edition* (Cambridge, MA: Harvard University Press, 1964 [1859]); Herbert Spencer, *Principles of Biology* (London: William and Norgate, 1864).

5   Peter Kropotkin, *Mutual Aid: A Factor of Evolution* (Boston: Extending Horizons Books, 1955 [1914]).

own set of laws but with enough correspondences between them that human society could be read as a continuously evolving expression of a unified whole.[6]

The theosophy of Helena Pavlova Blavatsky (1831–1891), which intrigued many anarchists, involved a teleology of divine evolution represented by successive "root races" whose finality was cosmic union.[7] Novelist Leo Tolstoy (1828–1910), a theosophist and anarchist who wrote a tract titled "The Kingdom of God Is within You" (1894), also admired Federov (1828–1903), who wrote that the common task of humanity was to use science to resurrect its dead fathers from particles scattered in cosmic dust.[8] Chulkov, Berdyaev, and Ivanov, contemporaries of both Fedorov and Tolstoy during the Russian occult revival, all posited a "mystical anarchism" that equated

6   See Sho Konishi, "Reopening The 'Opening of Japan': A Russian-Japanese Revolutionary Encounter and the Vision of Anarchist Progress," *American Historical Review* 112 (2007): 101–30, or his monograph, *Anarchist Modernity: Cooperatism and Japanese-Russian Intellectual Relations in Modern Japan* (Cambridge, MA: Harvard University Press, 2013).

7   See Helena Pavlova Blavatsky, *An Abridgement of the Secret Doctrine*, ed. Elizabeth Preston and Christmas Humphreys (Illinois: The Theosophical Publishing House, 1966).

8   See Leo Tolstoy, "The Kingdom of God Is within You: Christianity Not as a Mystical Doctrine but as a New Understanding of Life," in *The Kingdom of God and Peace Essays* (New Delhi: Rupa & Co., 2001), as well as discussion of Tolstoy in Alexandre Christoyannopoulos and Lara Apps, "Anarchism and Religion," in *The Palgrave Handbook of Anarchism*, ed. Carl Levy and Matthew S. Adams (Basingstoke, UK: Palgrave Macmillan, 2019). Regarding the "anarchist religion" inspired by Tolstoy in Japan, see Konishi, *Anarchist Modernity*. Regarding Tolstoy and the occult revival in Russia, see also Bernice Glatzer Rosenthal, introduction to *The Occult in Russian and Soviet Culture*, ed. Bernice Glatzer Rosenthal (Ithaca: Cornell University Press, 1997), 11, 22; James Webb, *The Occult Establishment* (La Salle, IL: Open Court Publishing, 1976), 157, 174–75.

political revolution with realignment in the cosmic sphere.[9] In England, union organizer and early feminist Annie Besant, who organized women matchmakers and fought to open the Masonic lodges to women, was convinced she was the reincarnation of Giordano Bruno, and it was theosophy that inspired her to fight for Home Rule in India. It was also through theosophy that she met Jawaharlal Nehru, himself a member of the Theosophical Society.[10] Just as socialists were attracted to the occult, spiritualists and mediums of all kinds, who were disproportionately women, were led by their spiritual views to engage the "social question."[11]

Further examples from the anarchist diaspora include the story of Greek utopian socialist Plotino Rhodakanaty, often credited as being the first European "proselytizer" of anarchism to arrive in Mexico, whose first task upon arrival was to draft a pamphlet titled *Neopanteísmo* (1864) while working with Julio Chávez López to foment uprisings in the Chalco Valley, after which he founded the Escuela del Rayo y del Socialismo, (which translates, somewhat ungracefully, as School of Socialism and Lightning [and/or] the Ray [of Light]). Inspired by Spinoza, Hegel, Fourier, and Proudhon, Rhodakanaty called his political pantheism "pantheosophy" and went on to form La Social, a sixty-two-branch network of agitators in contact with the IWA, who formed Falansterios

---

9   See Bernice Glatzer Rosenthal, "Political Implications of the Early Twentieth-Century Occult Revival," in *The Occult in Russian and Soviet Culture*, 196.

10 Andrée Buisine, "Annie Besant, Socialiste et mystique," *Politica Hermetica* 9 (1995); Peter van der Veer, *Imperial Encounters: Religion and Modernity in India and Britain* (Princeton, NJ: Princeton University Press, 2001), chapter 3.

11 Nicole Edelman, "Somnabulisme, médiumnité et socialisme," *Politica Hermetica* 9 (1995). See also Claudio Lomnitz, *The Return of Comrade Ricardo Flores Magón* (New York: Zone Books, 2014), 31–37, 271–75; Leda Rafanelli, *I Belong Only to Myself: The Life and Writings of Leda Rafanelli*, ed. Andrea Pakieser (Oakland: AK Press, 2014).

Societarios in indigenous communities.[12] Fifty years later, the politics of Ricardo Flores Magón (1874–1922) were immortalized in his newspaper titled *Regeneración*, while his comrades called each other "co-religionaries."[13] Further south, Augusto César Sandino (1895–1934) of Nicaragua (who later became the icon of the "Sandinista" revolution in the 1970s and 1980s), was enthralled by the Magnetic-Spiritual School, theosophy, and Zoroastrian, Hindu, and cabalist lore, fusing all these ideas together with communist ones in such a way that he was refused entry to the Third International—they had heard rumors that he flew a seven-striped rainbow flag alongside the red and black.[14] I could go on but do not have the space to treat so many complex stories of diverse colonial encounters with the attention to specificity they deserve. I merely present these few suggestive examples to remind us that the cross pollinations of diverse cosmologies underlying modern revolutionism does not necessarily stop, and perhaps find only their

---

12 See Carlos Illades, *Rhodakanaty y la formación del pensamiento socialista en México* (Rubi: Anthropos, 2002); In English, see John M. Hart, *Anarchism and the Mexican Working Class, 1860–1931* (Austin: University of Texas Press, 1978), chapter 1. See also Angel Cappelletti, "Prólogo y cronologia: Anarquismo Latinoamericano," in *El anarquismo en America Latina*, ed. Carlos and Angel Cappelletti Rama (Caracas: Biblioteca Ayacucho, 1990), clxxvii.

13 Lomnitz, *Ricardo Flores Magon*, provides a unique entry into the culture of the *Regeneración* press, briefly discussing Freemasonry (96–97), as well as the political influences of theosophy and spiritism among members; the reference to "co-religionaries" is found on 198. Regarding Magón and the Partido Liberal Mexicano (PLM), see also Rubén Trejo, *Magonismo: utopia y revolucion, 1910–1913* (Mexico: Cultura Libre, 2005); Eduardo Blanquel, "El anarco-magonismo," *Historia Mexicana* 13, no. 3 (1964).

14 See Donald C. Hodges, *Sandino's Communism: Spiritual Politics for the Twenty-First Century* (Austin: University of Texas Press, 1992), chapter 6.

latest expression in present-day anarchists' selective fascination with indigenous cultures and cosmologies.[15]

Not every anarchist was a theosophist or enamored with the occult. Emma Goldman, for example, wrote an entirely scathing account of Krishnamurti's arrival in America as the supposed theosophical avatar.[16] However, the fact that Goldman's *Mother Earth* and a variety of other anarchist periodicals bothered to criticize theosophy at all should tell us something—nothing is forbidden unless enough people are doing it in the first place. Even the skeptics often grudgingly recognized that they were kindred spirits. As anarchist C.L. James wrote in 1902: "However ill we may think of [Swedenborgian] dogmas, their influence is not to be despised. They have insured, for one thing, a wide diffusion of tendencies ripe for Anarchistic use. Scratch a Spiritualist, and you will find an anarchist."[17] Indeed it was none other than the president of the American Association of Spiritualists that published the first English translation of *The Communist Manifesto* in 1872.[18]

15 I explore contemporary anarchist solidarity campaigns with indigenous peoples movements in a more critical vein in Erica Lagalisse, "'Good Politics': Property, Intersectionality, and the Making of the Anarchist Self" (PhD diss., McGill University, 2016)," especially chapter 3: "anarchism's peasants and indigenous people fill a certain 'savage slot' . . . that has always served to justify anarchist politics whether or not real peasants or indigenous people are liberated in the process" (137). See also, e.g., K. Johnson and K.E. Ferguson, "Anarchism and Indigeneity," in Levy and Adams, *The Palgrave Handbook of Anarchism* for contemporary discussion (construction) of affinities between "anarchism" and "indigeneity."

16 Cited in Laurence Veysey, *The Communal Experience: Anarchist and Mystical Counter-Cultures in America* (New York: Harper and Row, 1973), 45–46.

17 C.L. James, *Origins of Anarchism* (Chicago: A. Isaak, 1902), cited in Veysey, *The Communal Experience.*

18 See Bernice Glatzer Rosenthal, "introduction to *The Occult in Russian and Soviet Culture*," 22.

We can imagine how much this annoyed Marx. But Marx's anticipation of a communist millennium after the overthrow of capitalism, brought about by a mixture of willful effort and inbuilt cosmic fate, isn't actually that different from the idea of the unfolding New Age. The major difference, and the one that prompted Marx and Engels to distinguish their utopian vision as "scientific" compared to the others, was their notion of the historical dialectic, which preserved the form, if not content, of the Hegelian one.[19]

---

19 See, e.g., Karl Marx, "The German Ideology," in *The Marx-Engels Reader*, ed. Robert C. Tucker (New York: W.W. Norton & Co., 1978 [1932]), 154; Karl Marx, *Capital*, vol. 1 (London: Penguin Books, 1990 [1867]), especially 494n4; George Lichtheim, *From Marx to Hegel*, (New York: Herder and Herder, 1971).

Occult Features of the Marxian Dialectic

Hegel's dialectic cast history as a dynamic manifestation of the Idea, the unfolding of consciousness itself, in which everything is but a mode and attribute of a single universal substance. Hegel's *Logic* (1812) features an obsession with emanation and return by way of neat geometrical constructions of all kinds, while in his *Phenomenology of Spirit* (1807), the Idea issues in nature, which issues in Spirit, which returns to Idea in the form of Absolute Spirit: in the beginning there is unity, and the differentiated world will only be complete once again when man properly beholds the totality in his consciousness. As Glenn Alexander Magee illustrates at length, "The dove of [Hegel's] Spirit emerges from God-created nature, and circles back to God."[1] Here we may remember Giordano Bruno, who wrote, "It is by one and the same ladder that nature descends to the production of things and the intellect ascends to the knowledge of them"; he further elaborates that, "The one and the other proceeds from unity and returns to unity, passing through the multitude of things in the middle."[2] For his part, Bruno's intellectual rival Peter Ramus insisted on a division between dialectic and rhetoric (ontology and language, or in

---

1   See Glenn Alexander Magee, *Hegel and the Hermetic Tradition* (Ithaca: Cornell University Press, 2001), 212.
2   From Bruno's *Italian Dialogues*, cited in Frances Yates, *The Art of Memory* (London: Routledge, 1966), 228.

Hegel: the totality and our beholding of it) and proposed that the "true art of memory is one and the same as dialectics."[3]

We cannot offer due attention to all details of Hegelian philosophy and its sources here, yet elaborate briefly on certain Hermetic aspects of his system of thought. Readers familiar with Hegel know, for example, that much of the discussion regarding "subject" versus "object" in modern social theory may be traced back to Hegelian philosophy, yet it is rarely discussed how Hegel's subject/object corresponds with *Corpus Hermeticum* 14, "For the two are all there is, what comes to be and what makes of it, and it is impossible to separate one from the other." Likewise, with Hegel's dialectic of desire and recognition in mind, consider *Corpus Hermeticum* 10: "For God does not ignore mankind; on the contrary, he recognizes him fully and wishes to be recognized."[4] It is also worth noting that Hegel's system of logic is a triad, each element further divided

---

3 Paolo Rossi, *Logic and the Art of Memory* (Chicago: University of Chicago Press, 2000), explains how Descartes, Liebniz, and Bacon honored a correspondence between words (*termini*) and things (*res*) (chapter 5; see also 61, 114, 191) and how Ramus proceeds similarly yet differently (98–99, 101). The direct quotes from Ramus are taken from Yates, *Art of Memory*, 233, and refer to P. Ramus, *Scholae in liberates artes, Scholae rhetoricae* (1578), providing discussion (231–42). Bruno called Ramus a "pedant," associating Ramus's interpretation with the Greek tradition, as opposed to his own, which was inspired by the spiritual insights of the Egyptians; see Yates, *Art of Memory*, 272. Yates suggests that Giulio Camillo started a historical-methodological-memory movement that Ramus rationalized by omitting images (239–41).

4 See Brian Copenhaver, *Hermetica: The Greek Corpus Hermeticum and the Latin Asclepius in a New English Translation, with Notes and Introduction* (Cambridge: Cambridge University Press, 1992), 33, 56; Georg Hegel, *Phenomenology of Spirit*, trans. A.V. Miller (Oxford: Clarendon Press, 1977 [1807]). In Yates's discussion of the *Asclepius* (Corpus Hermeticum II) in *Art of Memory*, she likewise elaborates on the question of recognition in the Hermetica: "When God created the second god, he seemed to him beautiful and he loved him as the offspring of his divinity . . . but there had to be another being who could contemplate what God had made and so he created man" (36).

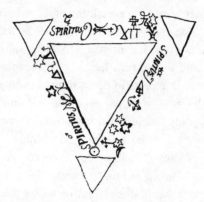

Fig. 9. Sketch by Hegel (the sides of the triangle diagram read "Spiritus").

into three chief moments, analyzed in turn into three other constitutive moments, which are split in turn into another three.[5] Finally, the broad observation is often made that Hegel's philosophy is pantheistic following Spinoza, and of course Hegel himself was also a Freemason.[6]

Marx breaks with Hegel in conceiving consciousness (the Idea) as inextricable from material social processes, rather than positioned as a first premise. Yet the material and the ideal remain indissoluble, Marx's logic is dialectical, and the Christian eschatology of his historical dialectic can be traced back to Joachim de Fiore as much as Hegel's can. And while one of the main defining attributes of anarchism is its anti-Marxism, many Hermetic features of Marxist thought remain preserved (as abstract content) as well as transcended within anarchism's concrete form.

---

5   See Georg Hegel, *The Science of Logic*, trans. George Di Giovanni (Cambridge: Cambridge University Press, 2010 [1812]).

6   Regarding the monism (vs. dualism) of Hegel's philosophy, see, e.g., Frederick Beiser, *Hegel* (London: Routledge, 2005). Regarding Hegel's relationship with Freemasonry, see Susan Buck-Morss, "Hegel and Haiti," *Critical Inquiry* 26, no. 4 (2000).

By this I of course refer to much more than dialectical logic itself, yet as long as we're fetishizing Hegel, we might as well go all the way. Marx distinguished his dialectic from that of Hegel as being materialist rather than idealist, yet in both of their systems the resolution of the dialectical contradiction comprehends not only the destruction and transcendence of the thesis by the antithesis but also its preservation. In Bakunin's system, however, the Positive and the Negative destroy one another entirely, leading to the transcendence of both, preserving nothing. Bakunin established the Negative as the motive force of the dialectic as opposed to Marx and Hegel whose dialectic began—and ended—with the Positive (thesis). Insomuch as Hegelian philosophy informed the political analyses and calls to action of each Marx and Bakunin, here we see one of the reasons they parted ways over the role of the state. Both Marx and Bakunin believed that democracy was the motive force of history, the real form of Hegel's world-historical Spirit. They also agreed with Hegel that Monarchy was the generic form of the state. Yet Bakunin sociomorphized the Positive into Social Reactionaries and the Negative into Social Revolutionaries. The state, as part of the (Positive) old order, would be destroyed and transcended entirely by the social revolution; no aspect of the existing society, including the state, would survive the insurrection. For Bakunin, this meant that "the state had to be *destroyed* in a general conflagration." For Marx, however, the essence of the state was democracy itself; he conceived democracy to be embodied in a constitution "hierarchically superior to other political forms," and therefore concluded that "the State had to be *realized* to its highest degree."[7]

---

7   See Robert M. Cutler, ed., *Mikhail Bakunin: From Out of the Dustbin: Bakunin's Basic Writings, 1869–71* (Ann Arbor, MI: Ardis, 1985) for further discussion, especially 18–21, (quote is on 21, author's emphasis).

Of course, the reasons why Marx and Bakunin came to different conclusions on revolutionary strategy extend beyond their diverse readings of Hegel. Bakunin's quarrel with Marx also arguably had much to do with elevating the revolutionary status of Slav peasants versus German proletarians, among other questions of social and historical context.[8] While Bakunin wrote of the peasantry, "They love the land? Let them take the land and throw out those landlords who live by the labor of others," Marx famously considered peasants capable of collective action only as much as "potatoes in a sack form a sack of potatoes."[9] As Engels wrote, "The Italians must still attend the school of experience a little more to learn that a backward nation of peasants such as they only make themselves ridiculous when they want to prescribe to the workers of the nations with big industry how they must conduct themselves in order to arrive at emancipation," while Bakunin responded by calling Marx "a Pan-Germanist down to his bones."[10] Bakunin also wrote elsewhere that the Russian people "are altogether democratic in their instincts and habits [and] have a great mission to perform in the world."[11] While anarchist transnationalism cannot be reduced to a function of patriotism, Carl Levy makes a valuable point here: "Even if anarchists and anarchism are assumed to be antithetical to nationalism and national movements, they, like socialists and the ideology of socialism (and even Marxism) lived in close

---

8   Here I follow Carl Levy, "Anarchism, Internationalism and Nationalism in Europe, 1860–1939," *Australian Journal of Politics and History* 50, no. 3 (2004).

9   Bakunin cited in Sam Dolgoff, ed., *Bakunin on Anarchy* (New York: Random House. 1972), 199; Karl Marx, "The Eighteenth Brumaire of Louis Bonaparte," in *The Marx-Engels Reader*, ed. Robert C. Tucker (New York: W.W. Norton & Co., 1978 [1852]).

10   Engels in letter to Cuno, cited in Nunzio Pernicone, *Italian Anarchism, 1864–1892* (Princeton, NJ: Princeton University Press, 1993), 53; Bakunin cited in Pernicone, *Italian Anarchism*, 47.

11   Bakunin cited in Cutler, *Mikhail Bakunin*, 21.

(one could say dialectical) relationship to both nationalism and the nation state."[12]

---

12   See Carl Levy, "Anarchism, Internationalism and Nationalism in Europe, 1860–1939," *Australian Journal of Politics and History* 50, no. 3 (2004): 331. For further analysis of the rivalry between Marx and Bakunin in the IWA, see Julius Braunthal, *History of the International, vol. 1, 1864–1914,* (New York: Frederick A. Praeger Publishers, 1967); Wolfgang Eckhardt, *The First Socialist Schism: Bakunin vs. Marx in the International Working Men's Association* (Oakland: PM Press, 2016).

Coda

The fact that Marx builds on Hegel who builds on the Hermetica does not necessarily mean they are wrong; it simply means that a vast amount of "rational" social theory relies on archetypes and geometries of thought stemming from a specific, historically situated cosmology—as does the notion of "rationality" itself.[1]

Socialism and occultism developed in complementary (as well as dialectical) fashion during the nineteenth century, yet the cosmological grounding of nineteenth-century anarchist politics is generally downplayed or treated as epiphenomenal in retrospect: just as Newton's alchemy is largely ignored in mainstream histories of the scientific establishment, so Fourier's law of passional attraction is rewritten in mainstream histories of the left as a vision of "a harmonious society

---

1   Beyond my own discussion, the reader may wish to consult the following in regard to the (co)construction of "secularization," "rationality," "science," "magic," and "religion": Peter Gay, *The Enlightenment: An Interpretation* (New York: Knopf, 1966); Keith Thomas, *Religion and the Decline of Magic: Studies in Popular Beliefs in Sixteenth and Seventeenth Century England* (New York: Penguin Books, 1982); Owen Chadwick, *The Secularization of the European Mind in the Nineteenth Century* (Cambridge: Cambridge University Press, 1975). My strongest recommendation would be to begin with Stanley Jeyaraja Tambiah, *Magic, Science, Religion, and the Scope of Rationality* (Cambridge: Cambridge University Press, 1990).

based on the free play of passions."[2] It was only when Marxist "scientific socialism" became hegemonic during the twentieth century that the theological understandings of modern revolutionism were buried from consciousness among the popular and academic left. The complex social, political, and historical reasons why certain currents of Marxism versus anarchism became more widespread (in practice and theory) during the twentieth century are largely bracketed here, yet note that contributing factors are necessarily overlapping and debatable, with explanations ranging from Eric Hobsbawm's, which beholds scientific Marxism progressively replacing the more "primitive" anarchism, to David Graeber's, which highlights how the centralizing logic of state Marxism was practical during the twentieth century of global war.[3] It is of course impossible to provide a scholarly analysis (representation) in this regard that is not also a (material) political position—Marxists and anarchists will at least agree on this particular point.

What is entirely clear, however, is that during this past century, whenever occult philosophy has been dealt with in its own right, it has generally been cast as "comforting" in anxiety-provoking periods of social change, or, in certain Marxian style, as a product of capitalist alienation. In Adorno's "Theses against Occultism" (in which he makes ample use of Hegel, however), occultism is both a "primitive" holdover and a consequence of "commodity fetishism" at once, in a typical circular (and colonialist) argument that suggests the occult worldview is wrong because it is animistic and vice versa—a "regression

---

2   See Peter Marshall, *Demanding the Impossible: A History of Anarchism* (London: Fontana Press, 1993), 149.

3   See Eric Hobsbawm, *Primitive Rebels: Studies in Archaic Forms of Social Movement in the 19th and 20th Centuries* (New York: W.W. Norton & Co., 1959); David Graeber, "The New Anarchists," *New Left Review* 13 (2002): 69.

to magical thinking."[4] E.P. Thompson, for his part, characterized the working class as "oscillating" between the "poles" of
religious revivalism and radical politics.[5] Over and over, occult
philosophy is portrayed as either inducing apathy among the
masses or as the territory of elite reactionaries who stir them
to hatred, rather than having any connection to socialism, communism, or anarchism. The symbiosis of Blavatsky's theosophy (involving "root races") with eugenics, and the association
of occult narratives and iconography with the rise of fascism,
for example, have also often been pointed out, and of course
the connections are there.[6] Here we may remember how this
story began, with a friend and comrade recommending that I
read *The Protocols of the Elders of Zion* (1903), a Russian forgery
in which capitalism is blamed on a secretive group of Jewish
patriarchs (who are in turn associated with Freemasonry and
magic). This book was widely distributed in the first decades
of the twentieth century—business tycoon Henry Ford himself
distributed five hundred thousand copies—thus playing a part
in fueling anti-Semitic sentiment in the years before the Nazi
regime and the Second World War.[7] It may also be useful for

4   Theodor Adorno, "Theses against Occultism," *Telos* 19 (1974): 8.
5   E.P. Thompson, *The Making of the English Working Class* (New York:
    Vintage Books, 1963), 391.
6   See Bernice Glatzer Rosenthal, "Political Implications of the Early
    Twentieth-Century Occult Revival," in *The Occult in Russian and
    Soviet Culture*, ed. Bernice Glatzer Rosenthal (Ithaca: Cornell
    University Press, 1997). For further discussion and sources in
    Laurence Veysey, *The Communal Experience: Anarchist and Mystical
    Counter-Cultures in America* (New York: Harper and Row, 1973),
    47n80; Nicholas Goodrick-Clarke, *The Occult Roots of Nazism: Secret
    Aryan Cults and Their Influence on Nazi Ideology* (New York: New
    York University Press, 1993).
7   See Victor E. Marsden, ed., *The Protocols of the Elders of Zion*, (Las
    Vegas, NV: Filiquarian Publishing LLC, 2006); Norman Cohn,
    *Warrant for Genocide: The Myth of the Jewish World-Conspiracy and
    the Protocols of the Elders of Zion* (New York: Harper & Row, 1966);
    Richard S. Levy, *A Lie and a Libel: The History of the Protocols of the
    Elders of Zion* (Lincoln: University of Nebraska Press, 1995). There

the reader to know that one of the first influential books to associate "revolutionism" (from the French Revolution to the Bolshevik Revolution) with a similar secretive directing force was *Secret Societies and Subversive Movements* by Nesta Webster, who herself relied heavily on the *Protocols*.[8]

The ideas offered within occult philosophy do not necessarily lead to revolutionary politics, yet they do not necessarily lead away from them either. When regarding the relationship of "magic" to anti-systemic movements, perhaps any deterministic formula is bound to fail. When approached by privileged persons with a lust for power, "magic" can serve to justify and advance elite aspirations. But without the influx of so much material charged as "ancient magical wisdom" that helped triangulate popular religion, modern materialism, and

---

also emerged works during this time period that did not partake of this particular view of history, yet wherein anti-Semitism nonetheless defines the analysis, such as Mircea Eliade, *The Myth of the Eternal Return: Or, Cosmos and History* (Princeton, NJ: Princeton University Press, 1974 [1949]), wherein the linear, redemptive history that has displaced (true) understanding of cyclical time is associated with Judaism. For an analysis of anti-Semitism with respect to the Saint-Simonians, see Zosa Szajkowski, "The Jewish Saint-Simonians and Socialist Antisemites in France," *Jewish Social Studies* 9, no. 1 (1947); compare with Jose C. Moya, "The Positive Side of Stereotypes: Jewish Anarchists in Early Twentieth-Century Buenos Aires," *Jewish History* 18, no. 1 (2004); Carl Levy, "Anarchism and Cosmopolitanism," *Journal of Political Ideologies* 16, no. 3 (2011).

8   See Nesta H. Webster, *Secret Societies and Subversive Movements* (London: Boswell Printing and Publishing Co., 1936). Other books drawing similar connections were also published around the same time, such as Léon de Poncins, *The Secret Powers Behind Revolution: Freemasonry and Judaism* (London: Boswell Printing and Publishing Co., 1929). While notions of Freemasons and Illuminati conspiring to effect the French Revolution had long existed, see, e.g., John Robison, *Proofs of a Conspiracy against All the Religions and Governments of Europe, Carried on in the Secret Meetings of Freemasons, Illuminati, and Reading Societies* (Dublin: W. Watson and Son, 1798), at the turn of the twentieth century we see an increased conflation of the Freemason and the Jew.

social discontent in new ways, we may never have seen the rise of "anarchism" as we know it. Even the quick glance at the history of revolutionism offered in these pages problematizes any simplistic dichotomy of New Age spirituality as reactionary (in both senses of conservative and right-wing) versus a materialist worldview as progressive (in both senses of forward-looking and leftist). Rather, secularized and "scientized" religion appears inherent to modern anti-systemic critique and collective action—the West's attempt to save itself from its impoverished materialism through an enchantment "newly reconfigured."[9] The world did not have to be "disenchanted" before modern antiauthoritarianism could occur, it had to be *re*enchanted: rejection of material exploitation, "materialist values," and materialist philosophy appear as three sides of the same coin.

---

9   See Thomas Laqueur, "Why the Margins Matter: Occultism and the Making of Modernity," *Modern Intellectual History* 3 (2006): 111–12; James Webb, *The Occult Establishment* (La Salle, IL: Open Court Publishing, 1976), 344–45, also makes this point.

Anarchism as a Historical Object: Attending to Questions of Race, Class, and Gender

At this juncture, the historical essay comes to a close, and we conclude with some discussion of the material presented as it may relate to practical political challenges of the present day. As I explained at the outset, I began this project partly in order to clarify, further to my previous ethnographic work, how the "atheism" professed by those working in the Western anarchist tradition intersects with a colonial mentality, as well as embodies a serious misunderstanding of the history of anarchism itself: maintaining a neat dichotomy between "spirituality" and "radical politics," only makes sense within a colonialist rubric wherein the religious Other becomes the constitutive limit of the "rational West." Beyond being "disrespectful" to a variety of (fetishized, exoticized) identities, insisting on a disenchanted universe delimits the radical imaginary in general.

Keeping this question in mind, I wonder what the eighteenth and nineteenth centuries in Europe would have looked like if militants regarded culture as property the way many anarchists and (post)colonial subjects do today—the question of "cultural appropriation" is an important one within contemporary social movements, and is arguably worth addressing in relation to the present discussion. Certainly the "occult" history of anarchism that I present above could be analyzed in terms of Orientalism, and of course the cross-cultural dialogues among heretics during the Crusades happened in the context of complex power relations.[1] At this time, however, it was not yet clear who would emerge as the dominant party. Is Kropotkin's *Mutual Aid* "culturally appropriated" because he was inspired by Japanese revolutionaries? Perhaps insofar as we don't know about it, in combination with the fact that there is now money to be made off Kropotkin-related commodities. Reading concepts like "cultural appropriation" onto the past, however, would falsely assume that the fields of meaning and value at the time can be equated to those inflecting today's self-making projects: during the Renaissance "difference" did not have the same currency, and people were not ascribed the same identities or "self-identified" according to the categories in play now. It makes sense that a critique of cultural appropriation emerges in the present-day context, wherein cultural difference is fetishized and certain people may valorize themselves by accessorizing commodified attributes of those they structurally oppress, but we may also lose something in the process of applying the logic of property to culture, and to spirituality in particular.[2] When entire cosmologies are reified as "proper" only to specific preordained identities, we are effectively saying they are false to the extent that they do not apply across the cosmos whatsoever. The sacred is thus rendered as alterity, nothing more than a cultural accoutrement in a marketplace as big as the universe. Appropriating indigenous spiritual forms without the intended content is entirely in line with the logic of capitalist colonialism, but so is marking off and containing everything considered sacred as *property* (and thus nothing more).[3]

---

1   See Edward Said, *Orientalism* (New York: Vintage Books, 1978).

2   For discussion of cultural appropriation, see Beverley Skeggs, *Class, Self, Culture* (London: Routledge, 2004).

3   Readers in anthropology might consider how the disciplinary "ontological turn" could be read similarly, wherein one (finally) grants the "reality" of plants that think or clouds that have agendas, but only by inventing multiple realities in the process: ontology

In other words, the fact that anarchists are often unable to recognize the subversive potential of religious sensibilities—whether those of indigenous women or of Bakunin himself—is disturbing beyond anarchists' failure to respect the "difference" or the "identity" of others, and indeed to recuperate such a debate within the parameters of "identity" and attendant proprieties is arguably racist in and of itself. As Jacqui Alexander asks: What would "taking the Sacred seriously mean for transnational feminism and related radical projects, beyond an institutionalized use value of theorizing marginalization?" It would mean that "the sacred would thus have to be taken as real and the belief structure of its practitioners as having effects that are real."[4] Or, in Gloria

---

(reality) becomes plural such that the white man can still enjoy his office without having to worry about the weather; see, e.g., David Graeber's "Radical Alterity Is Just Another Way of Saying 'Reality': A Reply to Eduardo Viveiros de Castro," *Hau: Journal of Ethnographic Theory* 5, no. 2 (2015); Zoe Todd, "An Indigenous Feminist's Take on the Ontological Turn: 'Ontology' Is Just Another Word for Colonialism," *Journal of Historical Sociology* 29, no. 1 (2016). Following Émile Durkheim, *The Elementary Forms of Religious Life*, (London: George Allen & Unwin, 2008 [1912]), the sacred is by definition and universally something "set apart." Rejoinders such as Talal Asad, *Formations of the Secular: Christianity, Islam, Modernity* (California: Stanford University Press, 2003) locate the "sacred" as a specifically Judeo-Christian concept. In either case, while most peoples throughout history do create categories of things, people, and ideas that are set apart from the mundane in some form, I here refer to the specific divisibility of the material and the "sacred" that occurs through processes of commodification and reification; see also Gloria Anzaldúa, *Borderlands / La Frontera: The New Mestizas* (San Francisco: Aunt Lute, 1987), 68–69, passim; Andrea Smith, *Conquest: Sexual Violence and American Indian Genocide* (Cambridge, MA: South End Press, 2005), chapter 6; see n13 below regarding the question of Smith's indigenous identity.

4   M. Jacqui Alexander, *Pedagogies of Crossing: Meditations on Feminism, Sexual Politics, Memory, and the Sacred* (Durham, NC: Duke University Press, 2005), 326, 327. Alexander's usage of "sacred" in her work is not entirely the same as my own (n3 above), yet our

Anzaldúa's less academic prose, instead of "surreptitiously ripping off the vital energy of people of color and putting it to commercial use, whites could allow themselves to share and exchange and learn from us in a respectful way," which for her means (sincerely) "taking up *curanderismo*, Santeria, shamanism, Taoism, Zen," not avoiding such traditions (as the private property of others).[5] Voiced one way or another, we all suggest the importance of actually considering the synergistic relationship between spirituality, faith, and radical political movements, whether in present-day Latin America or eighteenth-century Europe, up to and including the nineteenth-century "New Age" movement itself, with which modern anarchism coevolved.

In so doing, we also appeal to many present-day, self-identified anti-capitalists who do *not* take a hard atheist stance, yet who feel the need to hide their various spiritual inclinations in officially left-wing spaces: whereas at the turn of the twentieth century it was possible to say, "Scratch a spiritualist, and you will find an anarchist," a hundred years later the tables have been turned. Other things haven't changed that much—a zine an activist acquaintance of mine published in 2013 is titled *Anarchism and Hope*, wherein he advises: "Fuck waiting on someone else or some divine force to change shit. Hope means we can see how to do it ourselves."[6] Notably, the cover of the zine displays a circle-A symbol involving a discreet, yet, upon inspection, clearly stylized plumb line of Masonic iconography—quite possibly unbeknownst to the zine maker.

I also suggested in my introduction that the story told here is important to reflect on, because while the patriarchal

---

usages resonate (and differ in similar ways to those of Durkheim or Asad, in parallel, perhaps, to the gendered and racialized contestations over "sovereignty" discussed below).

5   Anzaldúa, *Borderlands*, 68–69, *passim*.
6   See Aaron Lakoff, *Anarchism and Hope* (Montréal: Howl! Arts Collective, 2013).

Fig. 10. Zine. *Anarchism and Hope* (Montréal, 2013).

bias of classical anarchist theory and practice is often noted in reference to the male proletarian workers' movements, the gendered quality of "anarchism" is arguably more fundamental than that. The masculine public sphere of anarchism extends back even further and articulates with an occult cosmology that is older still. As anti-systemic resistance in Europe shifted from the millenarian mode to modern socialism, the biggest difference was not, in fact, that the former was "religious" and the latter wasn't, but rather that in the latter the paradise of heaven would be manifest on the earth through the

Fig. 11 [Left] Mural of the Virgen de Guadalupe, cherished icon of
Mexican Catholicism (according to legend, she appeared in a vision
to the indigenous peasant Juan Diego in 1531). Here she is (re)claimed
in association with the Zapatista movement—wearing a *paliacate*, or
bandana, supported by an angel wearing a *pasamontaña*, or balaclava
(emblematic of the Zapatista movement)—and presented with darker
skin than in many official representations. Photographed in San
Cristobal de las Casas, Chiapas, 2011. [Right] Graffiti of the Virgen de
las Barrikadas (Virgin of the Barricades), another subversive rendition
of the Virgen de Guadalupe, this one popularized during the uprising
of the Asamblea Popular de los Pueblos de Oaxaca in Oaxaca (APPO)
in 2006 (photograph taken in Oaxaca, 2010). In Mexico as elsewhere,
popular religion and radical political movements often exist in
productive relation to one another.

works of men not God—indeed, men *as* God—and that it was the
job of a chosen few males who had access to "ancient spiritual
wisdom" circulating in new secret masculine orders to inspire
them to action. To simply argue now that "real" anarchism is by
definition feminist as well insofar as anarchism is theoretically
"against all forms of domination" does not engage the ways in
which the anarchist revolutionary person was constructed vis-
à-vis a variety of exclusions from the outset, especially insofar
as these continue unmediated by a certain unacknowledged
"vanguardism": revolution may be immanent in the people,

but as any anarchist around can see, fluency in a particular vocabulary, knowing the names of certain historical figures, and being vouched for by someone "in the know" is all requirement for entry into the anarchist club, as is a commitment to a specific ideological constellation informed by the history of its practice, wherein men's oppression by the state becomes the prototype for power in general. Of course, I may be forcing an analogy by saying that all of this social and subcultural capital resembles the "opaque system of signs" of nineteenth-century initiatic societies, but the (hidden) correspondence is worth reflecting on.[7]

Along these same lines, unless we narrowly define "vanguard" to mean "political party" per se, the common notion among present-day anarchist activists that Marxists are "vanguardist," whereas anarchists are not, does not bear scrutiny. Anarchists have always considered themselves purveyors of particular insight and continue to join social movements and the general fray to steer it all in a more revolutionary direction. To offer just one contemporary example, anarchists participated in the Occupy movement (2011–2012), despite its observed "reformist" aspects, to prevent it veering in a racist and nationalist direction and to steer it toward a liberatory politics.[8] My point here is not to criticize such a practice, but to suggest that its disavowal and dissimulation within discourses of mere "solidarity" may be disingenuous

---

7   See Erica Lagalisse, "'Good Politics': Property, Intersectionality, and the Making of the Anarchist Self" (PhD diss., McGill University, 2016), chapter 6, for discussion of the similarities and differences between the "security cultures" of subversive social movements of the nineteenth and twenty-first centuries, with attention to both different forms of internal organization and the different forms of state repression and surveillance faced by militants.

8   See, e.g., my editorial piece, Erica Lagalisse, "Participación e influencias anarquistas en el movimiento 'Occupy Wall Street,'" *Periodico del CNT* (Confederación Nacional del Trabajo) (November 2011): 383.

(if also, at times, tactically reasonable).[9] Similarly, while anarchists today carefully skirt the phrase "consciousness raising" (it sounds too Marxist), their various workshops on "anti-oppression" appear to have precisely such a purpose.[10] While there are significant differences between contemporary anarchist praxes and those of the eighteenth-century Illuminati, there are also obvious similarities. It is in the writing of Weishaupt that we see one of the first recorded references to the phrase "self-government," a favorite motto among present-day anarchists, who also generally consider themselves to be privileged guardians of an important "underground" tradition of subversive thought, one which they maintain as a discreet enlightened revolutionary elite during times of repression—indeed this idea was presented almost word for word by a keynote speaker at the Renewing the Anarchist Tradition (RAT) conference in 2008, to offer just one ethnographic example.

It should also be significant that today's anarchist intellectuals generally do not cite indigenous women scholars such as Audra Simpson, for example, when they are mounting their compelling arguments against the state: theirs are not the code words for belonging.[11] Rather, anarchist activists and scholars who are interested in questions of "sovereignty" often prefer to peruse the work of Giorgio Agamben, who, much like Carl Schmitt, brackets gender and race entirely by proceeding as

---

9   For further discussion in this vein, see Lagalisse, "Good Politics"; anarchist activists in the North America today often articulate their actions and ideology as "taking lead" from indigenous activists or other marginalized groups of people, yet they are also working within a tradition of their own.

10   See Lagalisse, "Good Politics," chapter 8, with respect to activist discourses and praxes of "anti-oppression."

11   See, e.g., Audra Simpson, *Mohawk Interruptus: Political Life across the Borders of Settler States* (Durham, NC: Duke University Press, 2014).

if one can equate "human being" and "male citizen of Rome or France."[12]

It is not simply sexist reading habits that marginalize indigenous women scholars' work but also the fact that their words, insofar as they draw links between politics and cosmology, are less easily recuperated within the European anarchist tradition, which has already decided that religion is bad, and whose model of oppressive power is the state. For the indigenous women in Andrea Smith's study, for example, "sovereignty" is "an active, living process within this knot of human, material, and spiritual relationships bound together by mutual responsibilities and obligations."[13] Audra Simpson, for her part, points out the "critical language game" involved

12 I refer to Giorgio Agamben, *Homo Sacer: Sovereign Power and Bare Life* (Stanford: Stanford University Press, 1998) and Carl Schmitt, *Political Theology: Four Chapters on the Concept of Sovereignty* (Cambridge, MA: MIT Press, 1985). Agamben presents the inclusion/exclusion of "bare life"/sexuality as fundamental to classical-then-modern politics without reference to gender, yet indulging de Sade and with prime reference to Foucault. The Holocaust concentration camp is presented as epitome of the "sacredness" (murderability) of life and modern bio/thanatopolitics by extension, Aimé Césaire, *Discourse on Colonialism* (New York: Monthly Review Press, 2000 [1955]) turns in his grave. Agamben crafts a certain genealogy of ideas wherein knowledge is the sovereign domain of European male philosophers in contradistinction to feminists and black scholars of slavery: in his work these are definitively excluded from philosophy qua philosophy in perfect symmetry with how Roman/French women and slaves are excluded (as "bare life") from Agamben's own analysis. See also Audra Simpson's rejoinder to Agamben, "One does not have to dwell exclusively in the horror of a concentration camp to find life stripped bare to cadastral form"; *Mohawk Interruptus*, 153–54.

13 Here and below I summarize arguments rehearsed at length in "Good Politics," see especially chapter 3. While Andrea Smith's indigenous identity is now hotly contested, it is nonetheless significant that her work has also often been ignored, e.g., *Conquest*; the quotation is taken from *North Americans and the Christian Right: The Gendered Politics of Unlikely Alliances* (London: Duke University Press, 2008, 260–1). See Lagalisse, "Good Politics," chapter 9, regarding the debacle over Smith's identity.

here: indigenous mobilizations of "sovereignty" are useful to signal "processes and intents to others in ways that are understandable."[14] These remarks certainly sound different than the definitions of "sovereignty" advanced by Schmitt, described by Agamben, and critiqued by many anarchists, wherein sovereignty is always an (unmarked, yet male) fantasy of absolute power via the state apparatus (and the practical project of consolidating this power as much as possible). But then again, why should Agamben or Schmitt be granted sovereign jurisdiction over the (power of) the Word? Indigenous women's mobilizations of "sovereignty" are not necessarily rhetorical, but even when they are, this is where the (performative) magic happens. Following their lead could teach us all something about "sovereignty" that Schmitt, Agamben, and their anarchist readers fail to notice: European "sovereignty" has always involved subsuming women and children as property of male citizens, whereas it is male citizens that are subsumed by the sovereign.[15] Furthermore, the male philosophy slip between (legal) person and human being is also preserved in the (dialectical) anarchist response—"autonomy."[16]

In lieu of fantasies of absolute state power, "autonomy" involves a fantasy of absolute personal power that must presume a strict independence of individuals (or homogenous groups thereof), which must then be mitigated by a correlate call for "mutual aid"—the other side of the same coin. Here we may also consider Anna Tsing's recent work on mushrooms

14 Simpson, *Mohawk Interruptus*, 105.
15 See Lagalisse, "Good Politics," chapter 9, where I elaborate this argument with attention to Lévi-Strauss's work on the universalization and particularization at work in combinations of linear and taxonomic hierarchy, Louis Dumont's theory of hierarchy, and David Graeber's rejoinder regarding the exclusion as well as subsumption that is involved in hierarchical arrangements, which I adapt with reference to Macpherson's work on the "possessive individual."
16 Beyond the summary reproduced below, see Lagalisse, "Good Politics," chapters 3 and 4.

and species interdependence, which proposes "mutualism" versus a falsely imagined "autonomy" in nature, thus striking a productive argument with the commonsense categories of Western anarchism without even meaning to. Tsing points out how the imagination of a species-being that is autonomously self-maintaining and constant across culture and history stems from a certain human exceptionalism: "Science has inherited stories about human mastery from the great monotheistic religions. These stories fuel assumptions about human autonomy, and they direct questions to the human *control* of nature, on the one hand, or human *impact* on nature, on the other, rather than to species interdependence."[17] In modern life science, the most important interspecies interactions were those of predator/prey in which interaction means wiping each other out. "Mutualistic relations," explains Tsing, "were interesting anomalies, but not really necessary to understand life. Life emerged from the self-replication of each species, which faced evolutionary and environmental challenges on its own. No species needed another for its continuing vitality; it organized itself."[18]

Anarchists, who followed Darwin on evolution and dabbled in theosophy's imagination of "root races," here follow in suit. Kropotkin's *Mutual Aid* (1955 [1914]) emphasized cooperation within species but did not focus on mutual aid among them. The anarchist ideas of autonomy, self-government, and self-management do rely in unacknowledged ways on the notion of "self-organizing system" of modern life science, whereas biology in the twenty-first century finds symbiosis the rule, not the exception, as do the natural science traditions of many indigenous peoples who predate Anna Tsing

17   See Anna Tsing, "Unruly Edges: Mushrooms as Companion Species," *Environmental Humanities* 1 (2012): 4.

18   Anna Tsing, *The Mushroom at the End of the World: On the Possibility of Life in Capitalist Ruins* (Princeton, NJ: Princeton University Press, 2015), 195.

considerably, in which "sovereignty" is a "knot of human, material, and spiritual relationships."[19] Yet the anarchist person is still imagined as an independent, autonomous, and transcendent (sovereign) being that enters into "mutual aid" with others of its kind, much like the modern person writ large—the state. And just as the state characterizes itself as benevolent to its citizens, the anarchist is benevolent to the people (women) similarly subsumed in his "autonomy" and without whom he could not survive.[20]

---

19 Tsing, *The Mushroom at the End of the World*, 199–200 (Tsing provides sources in recent literature on biology). In Lagalisse, "Good Politics," especially chapters 4 and 9, I discuss how today's anarchist activists continue to adopt political metaphors from the natural sciences, tinkering with developments in biology to articulate that the universe is on their side; e.g., many contemporary anarchists (and scholars thereof) discursively articulate nondeterminate systems to twenty-first-century anarchism, yet many who refer to nonlinear complexity and the Deleuzian rhizome as metaphors for their social movement activities are, in their everyday relations, still operating largely according to atemporal, linear algebras, a key example being activist praxes of "intersectionality" that involve projections of experience related to "axes" of oppression and their summation or multiplication.

20 Regarding women and the modern state, as well as feminist critiques of anarchism, the chapter "Women and the State" in Henrietta Moore, *Feminism and Anthropology*, (Oxford: Polity Press, 1988) is strongly recommended, as is Mona Etienne and Eleanor Leacock, ed., *Women and Colonization: Anthropological Perspectives* (New York: Praeger Publishers, 1980). Lynne Farrow, "Feminism as Anarchism," *Aurora* 4 (1974) and Peggy Kornegger, "Anarchism: The Feminist Connection," *The Second Wave* 4, no. 1 (1975) both indicate gender trouble related to the anarchist concept of "autonomy"; note that in Erica Lagalisse, "The Limits of "Radical Democracy: A Gender Analysis of 'Anarchist' Activist Collectives in Montreal," *Altérités: Journal d'anthropologie du contemporain* 7, no. 1 (2010) and Erica Lagalisse, "Gossip as Direct Action," in *Contesting Publics: Feminism, Activism, Ethnography*, ed. Sally Cole and Lynne Phillips (London: Pluto Press, 2013) I discuss the relationship of "second-wave" feminist critiques of anarchism to contemporary anarchist social movements, as well as the androcentric bias inflecting discussions of "egalitarian" societies in anthropological works commonly enjoyed by contemporary anarchist

Perhaps it should be no surprise that indigenous women's imaginations of sovereignty do not line up neatly with either the "sovereignty" or "autonomy" of the modern right and left or that anarchist academics ask me to authorize my texts by citing Carl Schmitt—they do want me to be accepted into the club and kindly offer me the password. Nor should it be a surprise that reviewers suggest consecrating my work with the latest exegetical ruminations on St. Paul by Simon Critchley, whereas it is possible to get through ten years of doctoral studies regarding the social history of the left and only find out about Rosa Luxemburg afterward because of a book that happens to be lying on Barbara Ehrenreich's kitchen table: anarchism has always been a gendered and racialized domain authorized by speculative elites as much as real builders.[21] In my view, when it comes to approaching things like "liberty" or "equality," the work of historian Jonathan Israel is more compelling than that of philosophers such as Agamben or Critchley, as Israel sets aside abstract propositions and instead works hard to "describe in the contexts of history and culture the actual emergence of these ideas."[22] Perhaps the anthropologist is

activists, such as Pierre Clastres, *Society against the State: Essays in Political Anthropology* (New York: Zone Books, 1987) and Harold Barclay, *People without Government: An Anthropology of Anarchy* (London: Kahn and Averill Publishers, 1982).

21 Simon Critchley, *The Faith of the Faithless: Experiments in Political Theology* (New York: Verso Books, 2012) does provide an in-depth analysis of the meanings of religion, sovereignty, and liberty in the work of Jean-Jacques Rousseau and left thinkers who follow him, thus offering an argument around "mystical anarchism" and faith that dovetails partially with my own; his own exposition advances by way of literature and logical propositions rather than an ethnographic social history. The book on Rosa Luxemburg I found on Barbara Ehrenreich's table (she had been asked to write a blurb for it) was Kate Evans, *Red Rosa: A Graphic Biography of Rosa Luxemburg* (New York: Verso Books, 2015).

22 Jonathan Israel, *A Revolution of Mind: Radical Enlightenment and the Intellectual Origins of Modern Democracy* (Princeton, NJ: Princeton University Press, 2010), x.

ERICA LAGALISSE

bound to favor historians such as Israel yet by the same token is left wanting if contextual analysis does not comprehend the interesting (and certainly productive) contradiction of ideas like "equality, democracy and individual liberty" actually emerging within new, secretive, status-restrictive, male-only clubs (often otherwise referred to, rather curiously, as the modern "public sphere"). How can so many of us pass over the (synchronic) gendered pairing of the Enlightenment salon and Freemasonic temple or the (diachronic) gendered series of ("magical") witches and ("rational") brotherhood ceremonies and yet claim to properly understand the form or content of the ideas of either? Not with recourse to the logic of "history," whether that of Foucault or Hegel (or the Hermetica itself). It seems all "earthly perspectives" are bound to be incomplete after all—including my own.

The Conspiracy of Kings: Attending to the "Conspiracy Theory" Phenomenon

The previous chapter synthesizes well-rehearsed material that I have elaborated at length elsewhere, whereas this second analytical discussion below concerns relatively recent research questions and involves more tentative hypotheses. One might say that my first analytical discussion is a summary presented to conclude, whereas this second is presented to begin anew.

During the decade that I researched this historical essay (2006–2016), the phrase "conspiracy theory" became increasingly common among my North American activist friends, as well as increasingly referenced by others among the intellectual elite. My "politicized" and academic peers look down on the uneducated and uncouth subject who falls prey to the "conspiracy theory." An increasing number of topics have come to be associated with the "conspiracy theorist." Ethnographically speaking—which is to say, by listening to people talk—almost anyone in North America, for example, may easily observe that critical interest in topics as diverse as national vaccine programs, the assassination of President Kennedy, and alien abductions is often discursively lumped together as part of a "conspiracy theorist" tendency. In 2018, the neologism "conspiracist" as a (derogatory) adjective is increasingly used as well, often by someone with left politics in reference to a supporter of President Donald Trump.

The people who use "conspiracy theory" and its derivations as epithets proceed as if there exists a set of criteria by which "conspiracy theory" may be defined. Presumably "conspiracy theories" rely on errant data. They attribute too much agency to high-ranking individuals or government agencies. Their adherents proceed in poor faith by lending more weight to information that corroborates their existing theories than information that calls their ideas into question. Contradictory evidence is taken merely as more proof of conspiracy. And so on. Yet if these were effective criteria, then the theory that Saddam Hussein possessed weapons of mass destruction (WMD), which served to justify the United States waging war on Iraq at the turn of the millennium, would be considered a "conspiracy theory," and generally speaking it is not.[1] In fact, there is no single (monothetic) principle by which "conspiracy theory" may be defined. Insofar as the phrase "conspiracy theory" has meaning, it resides in its function as a phrase used specifically to refer to popular (subaltern) ideas for the purpose of disqualifying them from respectable consideration.[2] Theories of conspiracy that are communicated by those "above" are not labelled "conspiracy theories," even if they are false and involve fantastic or incredible premises, whereas theories of conspiracy expounded by those "below" can rarely shake the "conspiracy theory" label once it has been publicly applied. We will return to this question.

Of course, it does remain the case that some ideas commonly marked as "conspiracy theory" are inaccurate—and

---

1   In this passage I follow Mathijs Pelkmans and Rhys Machold, "Conspiracy Theories and Their Truth Trajectories," *Focaal: Journal of Global and Historical Anthropology* 59 (2011): 74–75. According to polls cited in this work, 50 percent of United States citizens continued believing that Saddam Hussein possessed WMD even after it was proved otherwise, thus demonstrating a reluctance to alter views in light of evidence, a quality often attributed to the "conspiracy theorist" (69).

2   See Pelkmans and Machold, "Conspiracy Theories," 76–77, passim; Jack Z. Bratich, *Conspiracy Panics: Political Rationality and Popular Culture* (Albany: State University of New York Press, 2008), discussing "conspiracy theory" as a form of "narrative disqualification."

legitimately disturbing to those who seek to develop a broad-based anti-capitalist resistance movement. Some of these misguided theories have become very widespread and involve groups mentioned in this work—Freemasons, Illuminati, anarchists—inviting a certain commentary on my part. Indeed, as I mentioned at the outset, I have presented my historical essay on the "Occult Features of Anarchism" in the way I have partly to intervene in so much misinformation around secret societies, global power, and the Illuminati. I write to set the record straight. For this project to be effective, however, it is important to also highlight the kernels of truth that are mixed up with false information, to acknowledge the popular social commentary contained in many popular theories of global conspiracy.

As some of my readers may already be aware, a significant fraction of the videos currently found on YouTube that critics commonly dismiss as "conspiracy theory" tell stories of the Knights Templar finding secret treasure under Solomon's temple in Jerusalem during the Crusades, with Illuminati-controlled Freemasons later using it to collapse the great world religions into one big banking tradition in the name of Lucifer.

The scholarly historian may reject this story as a proper interpretation of events, and social scientists across discipline will of course prefer to highlight "systemic forces," rather than the whimsy of a few powerful knights and Freemasons, not to mention a few relatives of the Rothschild family, as per the prevalent anti-Semitic version. The popular story is clearly allegorical. As such it differs greatly in form and exposition from the one told by Karl Polanyi in *The Great Transformation*, for example, wherein global elites (and others following in suit) forsake traditional allegiances of tribe and country in the great, unprecedented project of modern banking borne of collusion, capitalism, and war.[3] Yet it should not take that much

---

3   Karl Polanyi, *The Great Transformation: The Political and Economic Origins of Our Time*, 2nd edition (Boston: Beacon Press, 2001 [1944]).

imagination to see how the "conspiracist" narrative differs more in form than content from scholarly history (being delivered, as it is, in a personifying genre of myth), and therefore its adherents could possibly be turned to a less flamboyant anti-capitalist analysis. Social scientists armed with the analytical tools of Claude Lévi-Strauss or Carl Jung or Jacques Lacan or Pierre Bourdieu (to name just a few) should be able to note in the popular account a certain critique of capitalist modernity, which students of Antonio Gramsci or Chantal Mouffe or Stuart Hall (to name a few more) might suggest trying to articulate with anti-capitalist social theory and social movements.[4] Yet while numerous North American TV viewers are fed stories of aliens building the pyramids of Egypt on the History channel, scholars have largely ignored such popular mythologies of power and history and have not properly studied the political economy of the current "Illuminati" cult ideology.

Scholars in social psychology, for example, often start from the premise that such "conspiracy theories" are simply wrong and spend research energies on explaining how and why its aficionados are irrational.[5] As for the

---

4   See, e.g., Claude Lévi-Strauss, *Myth and Meaning* (London: Routledge, 2005 [1978]); C.G. Jung, *Flying Saucers: A Modern Myth of Things Seen in the Skies* (Princeton, NJ: Princeton University Press, 1978); Jacques Lacan, *Écrits: The First Complete Edition in English*, trans. Bruce Fink (New York: W.W. Norton & Co., 2006); Pierre Bourdieu, *Distinction: A Social Critique of the Judgement of Taste* (Cambridge, MA: Harvard University Press, 1984); Antonio Gramsci, *Selections from the Prison Notebooks of Antonio Gramsci*, trans. Quintin Hoare and Geoffrey Nowell Smith (New York: International Publishers, 1971); Chantal Mouffe, "Hegemony and Ideology in Gramsci," in *Gramsci and Marxist Theory*, ed. Chantal Mouffe (London: Routledge, 1979); Stuart Hall, "On Postmodernism and Articulation: An Interview with Stuart Hall (edited by Lawrence Grossberg)," in *Stuart Hall: Critical Dialogues in Cultural Studies*, ed. David Morley and Kuan-Hsing Chen (New York: Routledge, 1996).

5   See, e.g., Martin Bruder et al., "Measuring Individual Differences in Generic Beliefs in Conspiracy Theories across Cultures: Conspiracy Mentality Questionnaire," *Frontiers in Psychology* 4 (2013); Viran

twenty-first-century anthropologist, while imagining he is on the side of the "oppressed," he too often eschews responsibility as a public intellectual, preferring to write in obscure venues about the "ontologies" of the ever-exotic colonial subject, while reeling away from fantastic cultural productions in his own backyard with all the force of an incest taboo. Or, when anthropologists do engage "conspiracy theory," they tend to focus on the sense-making functions of "conspiracy theory." Like Marxists discussing occult philosophy as "comforting" in anxiety-provoking periods of social change, social scientists often echo the hegemonic folk sociology that I discussed in my introduction, wherein "conspiracy theory" provides reassuring, simple explanations for unpleasant events that are difficult to account for. They are, of course, part of a long tradition that does have certain value. As Carl Jung elaborated with respect to the "flying saucer" craze of the 1950s, even if we do not find popular theories compelling, we may learn from them as modern myths, wherein the myths that characterize any given society (or subculture) teach us much about the adherents and their general concerns.[6]

More recently, anthropologists Todd Sanders, Harry G. West, and Paul Silverstein, for example, have all drawn a certain parallel between "conspiracy theory" and "witchcraft" as presented in the classical work of early anthropologist E.E. Evans-Pritchard, wherein they grant that "conspiracy theories" fulfill a certain social function (while avoiding any statement

Swami and Adrian Furnham, "Political Paranoia and Conspiracy Theories," in *Power, Politics and Paranoia: Why People Are Suspicious of Their Leaders*, ed. Jan-Willem van Prooijen and Paul A.M. van Lange (Cambridge: Cambridge University Press, 2014), who write that "conspiracy theories are a subset of false beliefs in which the ultimate cause of an event is believed to be due to a plot by multiple actors working together with a clear goal in mind" (220) and associate conspiracy theorists with "schizotypy" and "paranoid ideation" (228).

6   See Jung, *Flying Saucers*.

about their truthfulness).[7] Yet upon proper examination of a given popular theory, we may realize it actually communicates something of the everyday truth lived by its purveyor. It may be inaccurate to state that the survivors of a given high school massacre are merely "crisis actors"; on the other hand, working people are not entirely wrong in their general suspicion that the professional class is trying to kill them. Perhaps social scientists might grant more often that "conspiracy theories" happen precisely because the public notices that secretive government institutions are continually lying.

Instead, by both social scientists and activists widely applying the label "conspiracy theorist" and thus dismissing the rationality of diverse popular theorists a priori, no attempt is made to distinguish between theories that arguably involve valid lines of questioning ("Is it possible my child is sick because of the vaccine she recently received?") and those which are more obviously misguided ("Is the world banking system run by Jewish lizards or aliens or both?"). This is unfortunate, as it would seem that failure to intervene in the indiscriminate application of the "conspiracy theory" label to diverse theories arguably serves to foster a defensive identity among those ridiculed as "conspiracy theorists," encouraging empathy, solidarity, and exchange of ideas among those so

---

7   See Todd Sanders and Harry G. West, "Power Revealed and Concealed in the New World Order," in *Transparency and Conspiracy*, ed. Harry G. West and Todd Sanders (Durham, NC: Duke University Press, 2003), 1–37; Paul A. Silverstein, "An Excess of Truth: Violence, Conspiracy Theorizing and the Algerian Civil War," *Anthropological Quarterly* 75, no. 4 (2002). See also related discussion in Pelkmans and Machold, "Conspiracy Theories," 73, passim, illustrating how anthropological treatments of "conspiracy theory," including those cited here, betray a lingering functionalism. Note that Swami and Furnham, "Political Paranoia," offers an example of the folk sociological account as found within the literature in psychology: "conspiracy theories may afford individuals a means of maintaining meaning or control in their lives" (228).

labelled, such that persons who at one point merely stated that the CIA was involved in drug trafficking come to also believe in Jewish lizard bankers as well. I have not completed the formal and extensive longitudinal ethnographic research required to prove this, yet I have personally seen such a process unfold in multiple cases (often in triangular relation to YouTube viewing activity), which alongside a little common sense suggests to me that a broader pattern might prevail.

Facing a political landscape such as that of the United States in 2019, populated as it is with the "post-truth" of President Donald Trump and viral YouTube videos about the Illuminati being a group of politicians and bankers, rather than a group of revolutionaries who fought *against* the centralizing power of capitalist elites, important questions must be asked and interventions staged. My own modest contribution has been to write this book and concluding essay, yet it is insufficient. Concerned persons with left politics and responsible social scientists must proceed to ask further questions, such as: How has this topsy-turvy account of history come to pass? Who ultimately benefits from such disinformation? What might one do in order to disinform this false history and rescue the true legacy of left politics from those who would prefer we believe that the left was invented by a secret world government? Furthermore, when anarchist activists label newcomers to their social movement spaces "conspiracy theorists" and exile them on such a basis, what is really going on? Whose interests are ultimately being served by the activist policy of disengagement with "conspiracy theory"?

As I explained in my introduction, just as my original exploration into the "occult features of anarchism" was inspired by the clumsy solidarity of white anarchist university students in their dealings with Magdalena from Mexico, my concern around the "conspiracy theory" is largely informed by a decade of observing friction between university-educated anarchist activists who denounce "conspiracy theorists" and laypersons who defend them. And as with the story of Magdalena's marginalization, it is surely useful to provide a brief ethnographic example.

On an Occupy Wall Street email forum in early 2012, a newcomer to the listserv made a comment conflating the banker and the Jew. During the ensuing argument over the statement, the newcomer clumsily explained that he was trying to think things through, that he doesn't think *all* Jews are bankers or vice versa, but what about the fact that many are? Some non-Jewish listserv participants quickly proposed he should be cut off the listserv for racist speech that made participants feel "unsafe." Other non-Jewish participants then defended his right to be there, going so far as to say that "he has a point." Meanwhile, some Jewish participants on the listserv argued that it would be better to "straighten him out" than it would be to kick him off, which might, in the process, fortify his anti-Semitic tendencies. The first group of non-Jewish participants strongly disagreed, suggesting that conversing with such a "conspiracy theorist" would be a "distraction" that would derail more productive activities. Ultimately the newcomer was removed from the list. Significantly, the elite white participants who had defended the anti-Semitic new-comer ("he has a point"), yet who enjoyed greater quantities of social and cultural capital (they were well-known activists, had friends on the listserv, displayed higher education, and so forth) were *not* removed from the listserv. What is going on in such an instance? If activists were properly concerned about racist speech per se, then they should surely attend to the anti-Semitism of their friends as well as that of strangers. Instead, what we see here is a group of Jewish listserv partici-pants being ignored in the name of fighting anti-Semitism and scrutiny of the less educated newcomer, yet not of the well-positioned friend.

The contradictions here may be at least partially explained by my previous work that analyzes "good politics" among the North American bourgeoisie—it is unfortunately quite common for white activists of the professional class to mobilize the concept of "intersectionality" against one another in self-promoting performances of "anti-racism" and other forms of "anti-oppression," while ignoring the contributions of people of color and other oppressed groups in their collectives. I will not overly anticipate my analysis of this complex problem here, having offered it detailed ethnographic and theoretical attention elsewhere. But I do point those interested to my work "'Good Politics': Property, Intersectionality, and the Making of the Anarchist Self" and proceed to summarize very briefly.[8]

As readers versed in contemporary left politics in North America may already know, the notion of "intersectionality" was originally developed by black feminist militants and academics, both caught between racist white feminist movements and sexist movements for racial liberation, who articulated the necessity of approaching projects of both gender and racial liberation based on the "intersectional" experiences and analyses of racialized women.[9] My own analysis of the combined gendered and racialized marginalization of Magdalena in her

---

8   Erica Lagalisse, "'Good Politics': Property, Intersectionality, and the Making of the Anarchist Self" (PhD diss., McGill University, 2016) is available free online via the McGill University website or https://lagalisse.net/. Regarding the content summarized below, see especially chapters 7–9.

9   Classic references elaborating "intersectionality" include Gloria Hull, Patricia Bell Scott, and Barbara Smith, ed. *All the Women Are White, All the Blacks Are Men, but Some of Us Are Brave* (New York: The Feminist Press, 1982); Bernice Johnson Reagon, "Coalition Politics: Turning the Century," in *Home Girls: A Black Feminist Anthology*, ed. Barbara Smith (Latham, NY: Kitchen Table: Women of Color Press, 1983); Kimberle Crenshaw, "Mapping the Margins: Intersectionality, Identity Politics, and Violence against Women of Color," *Stanford Law Review* 43, no. 6 (1991); Chela Sandoval, "U.S. Third World Feminism: The Theory and Method of Oppositional Consciousness in the Postmodern World," *Genders* 10 (Spring 1991); Patricia Hill

own speaking tour is, for example, inspired by the compelling body of work on "intersectionality." Since the 1980s, the academic usages of "intersectionality" continue to shift, as do activist methodologies of "intersectionality." For example, many founding moments of "intersectionality" were one and the same, with calls for (white women) activists to work outside their "comfort zone," yet today's campus activists mobilize "intersectionality" to elaborate entitlements to "safe space." Also, middle-class activists now often ignore the "intersection" of class even though the theory of knowledge inherent to activist and academic praxes of "intersectionality" relies on the theoretical precedent of "class consciousness."

In "Good Politics," I explore these developments to suggest that campus activists in North America have preempted the black feminist challenge of "intersectionality" by recuperating its practice within the logic of neoliberal property relations and self-making projects.[10] We see, for example, that activist performances of "allyship" (to persons of oppressed identities) often consist in valorizing one's self vis-à-vis one's peers as a subject of "good politics" instead of constituting

---

Collins, *Black Feminist Thought: Knowledge, Consciousness, and the Politics of Empowerment* (New York: Routledge, 2000). See also Lagalisse, "Good Politics," chapters 5 and 9.

10 In "Good Politics" I discuss the homologies of propriety that characterize North American anarchist activist culture—that of the (neo) liberal self-proprietor, the proprietor of identity, and that of the static, closed, classical body whose (political) formation is always complete from birth, all atemporal versus processes of learning, growth, and dynamic imperfection. A common morphology is found among activists' tendency to privilege words over action, their subcultural sanction against emotive display, and the abstraction of experience into fixed and bounded identity categories: the value of abstraction over materiality, or transcendence over immanence, is replicated in part or in full within different orders of activity in both the ideological and physical domains of the activist game of "good politics," and this resonance serves to constitute and naturalize the game all at the same time.

tangible benefits for the persons with whom one is "allied": by "calling out" bad politics elsewhere, one garners good politics oneself. We observe that Bourdieu's theory of the transferability of economic, cultural, social, and symbolic capital, wherein class solidarity among elites is "misrecognized" in supposedly innocent estimations of "good taste" is ironically applicable to anarchists, wherein class power is rather laundered as "good politics" instead.[11] We see how proper linguistic framing translates into "good politics": for example, one may hear it discussed among activists that interrupting a racist comment with "Stop being such an asshole" is not "anti-racist," whereas the following sentence is: "I am not comfortable with your use of the word x because I feel it makes the space unsafe for people of color." Significantly, a sophisticated confessional deconstruction of not-acting or not-interrupting after the fact (e.g., "I realize what I did was sexist") may be considered "good politics," more so than acting without the proper accompanying speech. As a consequence, articulate students of Edward Said or well-spoken sexists may enjoy "good politics" simply because they cite and reiterate their bourgeois self-detachment ("reflexivity") by way of choicefully framed speeches.

We thus come to understand that in their calculations of "intersectionality" activists often subsume the "axis" of class under that of race for complex, interlocking reasons. These cannot be further explored here, yet I offer these provocative summaries as they serve to contextualize a related dynamic that is key to our current investigation: just as it is common to garner "good politics" by highlighting someone else's "bad politics," generally speaking, it is common for diverse professional-class activists to enjoy locating racism, sexism, homophobia, etc. among (diverse) working-class subjects (who have a relatively small presence in the milieu), as in this way they may take the critical lens off themselves. They naturalize their own

---

11   See Bourdieu, *Distinction*.

forms of racism or sexism by casting people living in poverty as the constitutive limit of "good politics." Such dynamics of self-valorization among professional middle-class activists would not be possible if activists held the experience of class oppression to provide "good, subversive knowledge" in the way they often suggest race and gender oppression do with reference to "intersectionality". Of course, following our discussion in the previous chapter, we understand that a nominal attribution of "good subversive knowledge" to those suffering racial or gendered oppression does not necessarily translate into practical power or respect enjoyed by actual persons with "intersectional" identities—often quite the opposite situation prevails. Yet it is significant to note at this juncture that in the everyday discourses of activists on North American campuses, the "working class" does not receive equivalent lip service.

With all of this in mind, what we see happening on the Occupy listserv above is not surprising. Rather, in light of the dynamics of bourgeois "good politics," this listserv scenario invites us to consider the extent to which imperatives of class respectability may play a role in leading professional-class anti-capitalists to ignore the "conspiracy theory" as a danger-ous "distraction" at the same time as they associate it, some-what ironically, with both a racist white working class and wrongheaded ethnic populations—"conspiracy theory" is a "white trash thing," except that it is also "common in the Middle East."[12] It may very well be that the phrase "conspiracy theory"

---

12 In my own ethnographic observations, activists tend to offer one or another of these contradictory explanations, somewhat in parallel with a certain tendency within academic research that attributes the "conspiracy theory" to either a specifically "American" mentality or a specifically "Middle Eastern" one, thus preferring racialized and cultural particularist analyses to broad comparative analyses or class analyses. See, e.g., Richard Hofstadter, *The Paranoid Style in American Politics and Other Essays* (New York: Vintage Books, 2008); Daniel Pipes, *The Hidden Hand: Middle Eastern Fears of Conspiracy* (New York: St. Martin's Griffin, 1998).

itself has come to function as euphemism justifying class exclusion within anarchist social movements. It is arguably no coincidence that as a university professor I may respectably discuss Central Intelligence Agency involvement in drug trafficking, yet a truck driver who says the same thing is often tossed off as a "crazy conspiracy theorist." And perhaps it is likewise no coincidence that wealthy white activists mobilize concepts of "intersectionality" and "safe space" against working-class participants who betray adherence to "conspiracy theories" with ironic reference to the importance of "inclusive" spaces, while allowing elite white anti-Semites to freely sound off. Surely it is significant that the working-class "conspiracy theorist" is nominally unsafe due precisely to his racism, and yet "anti-vaxxers" and "truthers" (persons concerned with national vaccine programs or investigating 9/11 as an "inside job"), who do not necessarily impute malice to Jews or other racialized people, are more quickly ridiculed and shunned from movement spaces than are elites who manifest racism in comparatively "respectable" ways.

Of course, it may still be argued that it is unpleasant to have meeting time consumed by discussions with theorists of conspiracy who are convinced the world is controlled by lizards from outer space. Yet shaming and evicting persons who betray an interest in a "conspiracy theory" from social movement spaces is also arguably problematic in the long run. Many measures suggest that there are more people in North America who believe in one or another "conspiracy theory" than there are readers of anarchist theory. Are anarchists truly interested in mobilizing people and their discontent into resistance movements? Or is the priority among activists to distinguish one's self as having "good politics" and protect their small, safe, social enclave?

Furthermore, and as suggested in my introduction, purveyors of "conspiracy theories" are often from subaltern groups, so the educated activists who generally state a nominal concern to "take lead" from "those most affected" by oppression should nominally allow for the possibility that the "conspiracy theorist" may actually be offering positioned insight. Beyond "tolerating" the theorist of conspiracy for the sake of reeducating him, activists' own ideology suggests that they might listen for subversive social commentary amid unfamiliar exposition. When activists instead immediately dismiss the subaltern "conspiracy theorist" as a problematic "distraction," we are invited once again to consider how the theories of epistemology related to "intersectionality" that activists proclaim within their social milieus are incoherent with actual practice, and ask why such a contradiction should prevail.

With respect to this question, and beyond the aforementioned dynamics of bourgeois "good politics" as a partial explanation, I am here tempted to advance a further tentative hypothesis: perhaps theories of "conspiracy" are rapidly dismissed by intellectual elites precisely because they uncomfortably highlight disavowed agency among persons of the professional class. Maybe members of the ruling class simply don't want to think about the fact that they do enjoy more power to affect institutional affairs than the janitor does, because then they would have to feel partially responsible for the workings of global capitalism (instead of blaming a sexist, racist, homophobic janitor). After all, only to the elite observer should it be surprising that persons in oppressed groups find the activity of dominant groups "suffused with intentionality" that elites cannot see or, to use the phrase of Pierre Bourdieu, "misrecognize."[13] Any orthodox historian is capable of illus-

---

13   The quote "suffused with intentionality" is taken from R. Brotherton and C.C. French, "Intention Seekers: Conspiracist Ideation and Biased Attributions of Intentionality," *PLoS ONE* 10, no. 5 (2015), which attempts to explain the irrationality of the "conspiracy theorist." Pierre Bourdieu explains his notion of elites "misrecognizing" their class interest within supposedly value-free observations in *Distinction.* Note that George E. Marcus suggests Pierre Bourdieu

trating that social elites only enjoy the power they do because they conspire to retain and accrue it, just as the institutional elites involved in the Holy Alliance or "Conspiracy of Kings" did at the turn of the nineteenth century. There is no politics without conspiracy. The question is simply "who" is conspiring to do "what."[14]

One feature of "conspiracy theory" oft maligned by elite observers is a suggestion inherent to many popular theories that global power functions as an entirely streamlined system, with total orchestration topping exactly one extremely pointy pyramid. It is true that social scientists could productively contribute compelling critiques in this regard. Pelkmans and Machold, for example, point out that the "most theoretically interesting field of conspiracy is theorizing that addresses conspiracies that supersede the 'petty' without extrapolating suspicions to a global scale."[15] In other words, we might produc-

---

himself approaches the paranoia of a "conspiracy theorist" for suggesting that elites have a collective class interest that is "misrecognized" in "Introduction to the Volume: The Paranoid Style Now," in *Paranoia within Reason: A Casebook on Conspiracy as Explanation* (Chicago: University of Chicago Press, 1999).

14   Here it is interesting to consider the work of Victoria Emma Pagán, including *Conspiracy Narratives in Roman History* (Austin: University of Texas Press, 2004); "Toward a Model of Conspiracy Theory for Ancient Rome," *New German Critique* 35, no. 1 (2008); *Conspiracy Theory in Latin Literature* (Austin: University of Texas Press, 2012). See also Kim Fortun and Micheal Fortun, "Due Diligence and the Pursuit of Transparency: The Securities and Exchange Commission, 1996," in *Paranoia within Reason: A Casebook on Conspiracy as Explanation*, ed. George E. Marcus (Chicago: University of Chicago Press, 1999); Kim Fortun, "Lone Gunmen: Legacies of the Gulf War, Illness, and Unseen Enemies," in Marcus, *Paranoia Within Reason.*

15   See Pelkmans and Machold, "Conspiracy Theories," 72, referring in turn to the work of Daniel Hellinger, who discusses "midrange" conspiracies as "operational conspiracies," in "Paranoia, Conspiracy and Hegemony in American Politics," in *Transparency and Conspiracy*, ed. Todd Sanders and Harry G. West (Durham, NC: Duke University Press, 2003), 204–32.

Fig. 12. Greeting card bought in Montréal (2017).

tively intervene by first granting that there are indeed many "pyramids" (plural, fragmented, and contestatory, of course) characterizing social space, and that the people at the tops are usually actively vying to stay there, whether they admit it to themselves or not.

The dismissal of the "conspiracy theory" is not explained simply by a politics of class distinction, it is also about rationality and how we understand power, yet it appears that here too

Fig. 13. Graffiti on rue Nôtre-Dame, Montréal (2012).

class informs our position.[16] The anti-Semitism within many popular theories of power is the most often stated concern among contemporary anarchist activists, yet ethnographic observation suggests that in their imagination the "absurd-

---

16   The classic reference regarding the class politics of distinction is Bourdieu, *Distinction*; see also Beverley Skeggs, *Class, Self, Culture* (London: Routledge, 2004) and my discussion of these works in "Good Politics."

ity" of the "conspiracy theory" is instead often attached to the involvement of what they call "supernatural" elements. As suggested earlier, here we see again how the presumed "irrationality" of suspecting successful political conspiracies (which indeed happen all the time) and the presumed "irrationality" of believing in aliens or psychic mind control collapse in the critic's mind. While popular thinkers develop allegories for capitalist extraction, wherein Jews, aliens, Templars, and Freemasons become protagonists in turn, the fact that UFOs and "magic" appear in some accounts is brought to delegitimize the larger popular search for understanding altogether.

In fact, insofar as we may discern a consistent substantial difference between the ideas commonly referenced as "conspiracy theories" and those commonly understood as "social theory," it is simply that social theory takes "society" as its unit of analysis, whereas "conspiracy theories" grant more power to individuals. More specifically, orthodox social theory generally involves a structural or post-structural theory of social change, wherein history unfolds due to relatively *impersonal* forces (e.g., Marx's "dialectic" or Foucault's "discourse"), whereas "conspiracy theory" appears to be judged as such partially due to a *voluntarist* theory of history embedded within, wherein the activities of individuals and groups can and do change the course of events. (This is Karl Popper's main grievance in one of the earliest published critiques, for example.)[17]

---

17 See, e.g., Karl Popper, "The Conspiracy Theory of Society," in *Conjectures and Refutations*, ed. Karl Popper (London: Routledge, 1963), 123–25; see also Charles Pigden, "Popper Revisited, or, What is Wrong with Conspiracy Theories?" *Philosophy of the Social Sciences* 25, no. 1 (1995); David Coady, *Conspiracy Theories: The Philosophical Debate* (Aldershot: Ashgate, 2006). Regarding Marx's historical dialectic and Foucault's "discourse," see Karl Marx, "The German Ideology," in *The Marx-Engels Reader*, ed. Robert C. Tucker (New York: W.W. Norton & Co., 1978 [1932])"; Michel Foucault, *L'ordre du discours* (Paris: Gallimard, 2004).

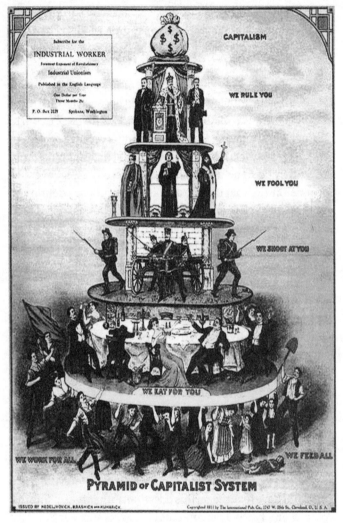

Fig. 14. The ubiquitous image of a pyramid topped with the "all seeing eye," represented most famously on the U.S. dollar bill and now found in both greeting cards and graffiti (Figs. 12 and 13 above), as well as many YouTube videos concerning Freemasonry, has become popularly associated with ("misguided") fans of "conspiracy theory," yet the pyramid has also been chosen in other times and places to depict the structure of power in modern, capitalist society, such as in this iconic image popularized by the Industrial Workers of the World (circa 1911).

Given that for decades now social scientists have cited Michel Foucault to elaborate the constraints of "discourse" and institutional power on their own range of thought and movement (while highlighting "resistance" among people living in relative poverty), perhaps the "conspiracy theory" is uncomfortable for the intellectual elite partly because it constitutes an anti-Foucauldian theory of power.[18] This is, of course, another way of saying that considering "conspiracy" among elites is uncomfortable for elites because it highlights the social power they do structurally enjoy and, therefore, inconvenient responsibilities that they do actually have. Chosen definitions of rationality and how one understands power, as well as one's proclivity toward an impersonal (structural) versus personal (voluntarist) understanding of history, do appear related to social class, wherein both elite and the popular theorists enjoy different insights and suffer different blind spots.

I invite all politically engaged readers, both activists and academics, to rearrange and play with the questions opened up here in critically productive ways. Given the current prevalence of the phrase "conspiracy theory" and its diverse and proliferating contents, it is important for us to properly explore how opposing arguments on either side of "conspiracy theory" debates are defined by distinct a priori premises regarding history and causality, as well as different forms of argumentation and exposition, and how the vastly different epistemologies in play as activists "talk past each other" about "conspiracy" appear related to differences of class culture, interest, and subjectivity. I have focused on this question, rather than using this space to simply scold the contents of various amateur YouTube videos on Freemasonry (which would be succumbing to the

---

18   Of course, many scholars who cite Foucault in such a fashion do so inaccurately, i.e., the commonsense "Foucauldian theory of power" I present here is to be understood as an ethnographic, sociological phenomenon.

elite predisposition I discuss), as it seems more important to explore why so many participants recently involved in leftist activism and scholarship have not actively worked to challenge the increasingly popular idea that the left (in general) and the Illuminati (in particular) are one and the same with a secret world government.

Since the election of Donald Trump in the United States in 2016, persons involved in left politics have been aghast at the overwhelming number of neofascist groups parroting the anti-Semitic ideas found in the *Protocols of the Elders of Zion*, yet such a scenario was not entirely unpredictable. As I pointed out in my introduction, the analysis of the Occupy movement provided on YouTube by David Icke (purveyor of the lizard banker hypothesis) enjoyed more "views" than almost all activist produced videos concerning Occupy combined.[19] Yet it seems that during the past decade many persons involved in left politics have cared more about keeping their own hands respectably clean, scoffing at the "conspiracy theory" from a distance, than about preventing damaging disinformation, including theories of history that inspire and justify the growing neofascist movements in North America today. This scenario alone is enough reason to begin seriously hypothesizing the "conspiracy theory" in relation to the making and unmaking of class respectability, whereby some ideas are made polluted by a constructed association with others, and wherein people are made polluted by and pollute ideas via the same chain of associations.

Going forward, anti-capitalists of all stripes would do well to properly tackle the abundant and curious confusion

---

19 See David Icke, *Essential Knowledge for a Wall Street Protestor* (2011), accessed July 20, 2018, https://www.youtube.com/watch?v=gV9A2lGShuk. For discussion of David Icke, see Tyson Lewis and Richard Kahn, "The Reptoid Hypothesis: Utopian and Dystopian Representational Motifs in David Icke's Alien Conspiracy Theory," *Utopian Studies* 16, no. 1 (2005).

regarding the left and the Conspiracy of Kings, the disturbing racialized political imaginaries, and the plethora of "bizarre" origin stories of capitalism often found within the works marked "conspiracy theory." I hope this book may come in useful to that end. I hope that some persons identified as "conspiracy theorists" read it and feel both productively challenged and validated by my words. Being written in elite genre, it will also likely be read by the sort of professional middle-class subject who generally disdains the "conspiracy theory," wherein the utility of the work will depend entirely on how these readers themselves decide to use it. Hopefully they will use the information acquired to engage with diverse "conspiracy theorists" in public forums and everyday life. Rather than disdaining from a distance the millions of people who fear an Illuminati-controlled "New World Order," perhaps they might engage in substantive argument with them, using some of the facts provided in this this work in the process. They might discuss with them how the new neoliberal world order is indeed controlled by conspiring elites, including bankers, yet the bankers are not specifically Jewish or lizards nor associated with the Illuminati. They might explain further how it serves the real "blue-blooded" parasites in power to have people believe that they are.

Of course, it is here that a true conspiracy may exist. Indeed it would be irresponsible to discuss the topic of the "conspiracy theory" as much as I have without attending to the fact that the Central Intelligence Agency of the United States has specifically worked to promote the category in the media—this fact having been duly researched and established in peer reviewed academic literature, something I feel I must mention, lest I be tarnished as a "conspiracy theorist" myself.[20] The fact that the CIA has promoted the concept of the

---

20 See Lance deHaven-Smith, *Conspiracy Theory in America* (Austin: University of Texas Press, 2013).

"conspiracy theory" and potentially contributed to its media content does not mean, following a certain misguided logic often attributed to "conspiracy theory," that the CIA "invented" the conspiracy theory or is the sole or primary "cause" of the "conspiracy theory," which is the outcome of diverse and combined historical and cultural forces. The *Protocols of the Elders of Zion* was published at the turn of the twentieth century, and various books that associated left politics with a secret world government were published around the same time, long before the CIA existed.[21] Yet every social scientist is capable of understanding that a government agency may have a vested interest in promoting existing ideas that distract from true government corruption and violence, including those of the increasingly global oligarchy currently enforcing neoliberal austerity programs (predatory capitalist extraction) throughout the world.

Of course, in tackling the misinformation in certain popular theories of conspiracy, both scholars and activists must also concentrate on factors beyond possible government involvement. While we must always be vigilant to not reify a "conspiracy theory" or the "conspiracy theorist," there are certain forms of cultural production associated with certain theories of conspiracy—YouTube videos about the secret order of the Illuminati, for example—whose consumption and crafting are seductive to persons of some demographics more than others. Aficionados do not solely include the disaffected white man "living in his mother's basement," as per the stereotype discussed in my introduction, yet it is clear that certain recurring motifs, rhetorical styles, and cinematographic elements in these videos invite us to perceive a genre, which we may then analyze in terms of race, class, gender, and cultural context, paying attention to questions of allegory and archetype, narrative and imagery, voice and public, authorship and audience,

21 See, e.g., the sources cited in "Coda", 73n8, in this work.

for the purpose of practical intervention. In the process, we might also explore how both dominant powers and critical "conspiracy theorist" artists make use of occult(ed) "arts of memory" to compel their publics, and thus how Renaissance magic arguably continues to inform both right and left in the twenty-first century, albeit not in the way some "conspiracy theorists" may suspect.

As discussed earlier in this work, the Classical "art of memory" was largely absorbed into the science of nature, yet it also perseveres throughout the modern world in other applications. Patriotic statues bearing personified images of the nation, decorated with emblems and amid arches of imposing architecture, for example, are clearly designed to impress particular collective identities upon the memory. Both mainstream media conglomerates and creators of YouTube videos concerning great conspiracies of global power also make use of psychologically compelling visual techniques. Both include images that are "wondrous, personify, and involve action or unfamiliar combinations" as per the Classical mnemonic art, which may work insofar as it mobilizes important insights into the workings of human cognition.[22] Perhaps we do well to end this essay with suggestive questions along precisely these lines. Indeed, it may be worthwhile exploring how one of the modern schools that contains and transcends the Renaissance arts of memory is Freudian psychoanalysis: the unity of the

---

22 Suggestive patterns among multiple arts of memory in diverse cultures imply that there may be a (necessary) connection between classification and inference on one hand and evocation, ideation, and poetic imagination on the other; see Pablo Rossi, *Logic and the Art of Memory* (Chicago: University of Chicago Press, 2000); Carlo Severi, *The Chimera Principle: An Anthropology of Memory and Imagination* (Chicago: Hau, 2015). Severi studies the iconographies of indigenous societies to propose, for example, that "counterintuitive graphic representations" (often chimeras that "one might consider to be *imagenes agentes*") are a key aspect of many non-Western arts of memory (20, passim; see also chapter 1).

heavens yields to the unity of the self. And as metaphysics yields to psychology, "memory as a key to magic was displaced by memory as a key to soul-searching."[23] For Freud, memories were largely personal affairs (the universal archetypes of Giordano Bruno and Carl Jung being de-emphasized), yet his project likewise rested upon a faith that we have the capacity to recover all forgotten experience and thus make the record of human history whole.[24] Meanwhile, it was Freud's nephew Edward Bernays, author of works such as "Propaganda" (1928) and "Engineering Consent" (1947), who played a key role in inventing the emotionally manipulative, image-based commercial advertisement, as well as "public relations" as a field broadly speaking.[25] Indeed, the occult(ed) crafts discussed in these pages may equally inspire the psychological machinations of modern advertising and social media, as well as the fantasies of fascism, the apocalypse of the dialectic, and the anarchist faith in an egalitarian social order. We would be wise

---

23 See, e.g., Patrick H. Hutton, "The Art of Memory Reconceived: From Rhetoric to Psychoanalysis," *Journal of the History of Ideas* 48, no. 3 (1987). Hutton analyzes how the art of memory (re)surfaces in the Romantic period, when a growing interest in the dynamics of human development from infancy to adulthood (and therefore autobiography) provided a "sense of unity that could no longer be found in the heavens" (380) and how the technique of soul-searching in the Romantic tradition culminates in psychoanalysis; "The notion of the life process as a structured sequence of discrete units demarcated by crises of transition would provide the architectonics for a new art of memory devoted to self-analysis" (385).

24 See Hutton, "The Art of Memory Reconceived"; "Like Bruno, [Freud] was in search of a model that would enable him to uncover a secret universe" (386); a central proposition of Freud's theory of "screen memories" is that images are substituted for ideas (387–88). If the analyses of screen memories can disclose lost experiences of childhood, then analysis of the myths of "primitive peoples" may recover lost memories of human origins (389).

25 See Edward Bernays, *Propaganda* (New York: Kennikat Press, 1972 [1928]); Edward Bernays, *The Engineering of Consent* (Norman: University of Oklahoma Press, 1955).

to not ignore their power, because now, as during the nineteenth century, as during the Renaissance period with which this essay began, the Hermetica proves "adaptable to a variety of projects," including both pyramid and levelling schemes, as well as pyramid schemes for levelling—As Above, So Below.

Acknowledgments

Great thanks go to Adrián Hiram Gutiérrez Benítez, who has inspired and supported my studies in the social history of "magic" for many years now. I am especially grateful as well to my friend Clara-Swan Kennedy, who provided invaluable research assistance and moral support during the years of research and writing, and to David Graeber, who encouraged me to develop this essay during the long decade of my doctoral studies.

The historical research presented in this work was first drafted in 2009 as a qualifying essay for PhD candidacy in the Department of Anthropology at McGill University, supervised by Dr. Catherine Legrand, chair of the History Department, and my PhD supervisor Dr. Kristin Norget, professor in anthropology. A version of this essay was also rehearsed as chapter 3 of my PhD dissertation, "'Good Politics': Property, Intersectionality, and the Making of the Anarchist Self," defended at McGill University (2015), thus benefitting from the interdisciplinary reading and review of my PhD defense committee, including Dr. John Galaty and Dr. André Costopoulos of the Anthropology Department, Dr. William Clare Roberts of the Political Science Department, and my two external examiners, Dr. Beverley Skeggs of the Sociology Department of Goldsmiths University of London and Dr. Gabriella Coleman of the McGill Department of Art History and Communications Studies. Among this team, I extend special thanks to André Costopoulos for his support and interest in this work during its formative stages, to Biella Coleman for her helpful feedback on the draft manuscript, and to Bev Skeggs who later became my postdoctoral research supervisor at the London School of Economics (2018–2019) and supported the crafting of this book in that capacity. I also wish to thank Dr. Setrag Manoukian of the McGill Anthropology Department, who contributed a helpful reading of an early draft of the historical essay in 2013, and who has since helped me think through the conundrums of "conspiracy theory." Dr. Jerome Rousseau of the McGill University Anthropology Department offered a close reading of a near-final draft in 2018, helping me to clarify and improve the text.

The historical essay was also presented as a work in progress at the Anarchist Studies Network (ASN) conference in Loughborough, UK, in 2012, where many anarchist scholars and scholars of anarchism generously offered constructive feedback and support. In particular I thank Dr. Jamie Heckert for his longstanding and heartfelt encouragement in this project, as well as the enthusiastic support and guidance of Dr. Carl Levy of the Department of Politics and International Relations at Goldsmiths University of London, whose research on the social history of anarchism has been an inspiration for my own.

The essay was subsequently developed as a chapter contribution to *Essays on Anarchism and Religion*, vol. 2, edited by Dr. Alexandre Christoyannopoulos and Dr. Matthew Adams. I strongly thank both Alex and Matt for their ongoing support throughout the (rather long) review process, first involving two anonymous peer reviewers organized by Open Books Press, and then another pair of anonymous peer reviewers years later organized by Stockholm University Press, all four of whom contributed crucial insights and important advice.

I thank the Fonds Québécois pour le recherche—Société et culture, the Social Sciences and Humanities Research Council of Canada, and the U.S.-Canada program of the Fulbright

Foundation, who together funded the research leading to this book.

Finally, I would like to thank the many librarians who helped along the way, including the interlending and archival librarians of the London School of Economics (LSE), the archivists at the International Institute of Social History (IISH) in Amsterdam, the librarians at the Warburg Institute of the University of London, and the interlibrary loans librarians of McGill University Library, who sometimes got into the spirit of things with replies such as: "It seems Robison's Proofs of a Conspiracy against All the Religions and Governments of Europe (1798) has gone missing from the Rare Books section.... It must be a conspiracy :-)."

Bibliography

Adorno, Theodor. "Theses against Occultism." *Telos* 19 (1974).

Agamben, Giorgio. *Homo Sacer: Sovereign Power and Bare Life.* Stanford: Stanford University Press, 1998.

Alexander, M. Jacqui. *Pedagogies of Crossing: Meditations on Feminism, Sexual Politics, Memory, and the Sacred.* Durham, NC: Duke University Press, 2005.

Anidjar, Gil. "Secularism." *Critical Inquiry* 33, no. 1 (2006): 52–76.

Anzaldúa, Gloria. *Borderlands / La Frontera: The New Mestiza.* San Francisco: Aunt Lute, 1987.

Arnold, Paul. *Histoire des Rose-Croix et les origines de la franc-maçonnerie.* Paris: Mercure de France, 1955.

Asad, Talal. *Formations of the Secular: Christianity, Islam, Modernity.* California: Stanford University Press, 2003.

Bakunin, Michael. "God and the State." In *God and the State: With a New Introduction and Index of Persons.* Edited by Paul Avrich. New York: Dover Publications Inc., 1970.

Barclay, Harold. "Anarchist Confrontations with Religion." In *New Perspectives on Anarchism.* Edited by Nathan Jun and Shane Wahl, 169–88. Lanham: Lexington Books, 2010.

———. *People without Government: An Anthropology of Anarchy.* London: Kahn and Averill Publishers, 1982.

Beiser, Frederick. *Hegel.* London: Routledge, 2005.

Benz, Ernst. *The Theology of Electricity.* Translated by Wolfgang Taraba. Allison Park, PA: Pickwick Publications, 1989.

Bernays, Edward. *The Engineering of Consent.* Norman: University of Oklahoma Press, 1955.

———. *Propaganda.* New York: Kennikat Press, 1972 [1928].

Blanquel, Eduardo. "El anarco-magonismo." *Historia Mexicana* 13, no. 3 (1964): 394–427.

Blavatsky, Helena Pavlova. *An Abridgement of the Secret Doctrine*. Edited by Elizabeth Preston and Christmas Humphreys. Illinois: The Theosophical Publishing House, 1966.

Bose, Atindranath. *A History of Anarchism*. Calcutta: World Press, 1967.

Bourdieu, Pierre. *Distinction: A Social Critique of the Judgement of Taste*. Cambridge, MA: Harvard University Press, 1984.

Bratich, Jack Z. *Conspiracy Panics: Political Rationality and Popular Culture*. Albany: State University of New York Press, 2008.

Braunthal, Julius. *History of the International: Vol. 1, 1864–1914*. New York: Frederick A. Praeger Publishers, 1967.

Brotherton, R., and C.C. French. "Intention Seekers: Conspiracist Ideation and Biased Attributions of Intentionality." *PLoS ONE* 10, no. 5 (2015).

Bruder, Martin, Peter Haffke, Nick Neave, Nina Nouripanah, and Roland Imhoff. "Measuring Individual Differences in Generic Beliefs in Conspiracy Theories across Cultures: Conspiracy Mentality Questionnaire." *Frontiers in Psychology* 4 (2013): 1–15.

Buck-Morss, Susan. "Hegel and Haiti." *Critical Inquiry* 26, no. 4 (Summer 2000): 821–65.

Buisine, Andrée. "Annie Besant, socialiste et mystique." *Politica Hermetica* 9 (1995).

Burke, Peter. *Popular Culture in Early Modern Europe*. Cambridge: Cambridge University Press, 1978.

Campion, Leo. *Le drapeau noir, l'équerre et le compas*. Marseille: Editions Culture et Liberté, 1969.

Cappelletti, Angel. "Prólogo y cronologia: anarquismo latinoamericano." In *El anarquismo en America Latina*. Edited by Carlos and Angel Cappelletti Rama, ix–ccxvii. Caracas: Biblioteca Ayacucho, 1990.

Césaire, Aimé. *Discourse on Colonialism*. New York: Monthly Review Press, 2000 [1955].

Chadwick, Owen. *The Secularization of the European Mind in the Nineteenth Century (the Gifford Lectures in the University of Edinburgh for 1973–4)*. Cambridge: Cambridge University Press, 1975.

Christoyannopoulos, Alexandre, and Lara Apps. "Anarchism and Religion." In *The Palgrave Handbook of Anarchism*. Edited by Carl Levy and Matthew Adams. Basingstoke, UK: Palgrave Macmillan, 2019.

Clastres, Pierre. *Society against the State: Essays in Political Anthropology*. New York: Zone Books, 1987.

Coady, David. *Conspiracy Theories: The Philosophical Debate.* Aldershot: Ashgate, 2006.

Cohn, Norman. *The Pursuit of the Millennium: Revolutionary Millenarians and Mystical Anarchists of the Middle Ages.* Oxford: Oxford University Press, 1970.

———. *Warrant for Genocide: The Myth of the Jewish World-Conspiracy and the Protocols of the Elders of Zion.* New York: Harper & Row, 1966.

Collins, Patricia Hill. *Black Feminist Thought: Knowledge, Consciousness, and the Politics of Empowerment.* 2nd rev. 10th anniversary ed. New York: Routledge, 2000.

Combes, André. *Les trois siècles de la franc-Maçonnerie française.* Paris: Dervy, 2006.

Copenhaver, Brian. *The Book of Magic: From Antiquity to Enlightenment.* New York: Penguin Books, 2015.

———. *Hermetica: The Greek Corpus Hermeticum and the Latin Asclepius in a New English Translation, with Notes and Introduction.* Cambridge: Cambridge University Press, 1992.

Couturat, Louis. *La logique de Leibniz: d'après les documents inédits.* Paris: Félix Alcan, 1901.

Crenshaw, Kimberle. "Mapping the Margins: Intersectionality, Identity Politics, and Violence against Women of Color." *Stanford Law Review* 43, no. 6 (1991): 1241–99.

Critchley, Simon. *The Faith of the Faithless: Experiments in Political Theology.* New York: Verso Books, 2012.

Cutler, Robert M., ed. *Mikhail Bakunin: From Out of the Dustbin: Bakunin's Basic Writings, 1869–71.* Ann Arbor, MI: Ardis, 1985.

Darwin, Charles. *On the Origin of Species: A Facsimile of the First Edition.* Cambridge, MA: Harvard University Press, 1964 [1859].

de Poncins, Léon. *The Secret Powers Behind Revolution: Freemasonry and Judaism.* London: Boswell Printing and Publishing Co., 1929.

deHaven-Smith, Lance. *Conspiracy Theory in America.* Austin: University of Texas Press, 2013.

Dolgoff, Sam, ed. *Bakunin on Anarchy.* New York: Random House, 1972.

Doyle, William. *The Parlementaires of Bordeaux at the End of the Eighteenth Century, 1775–1790.* PhD diss., Oxford University, 1967.

Dubreuil, J.P. *Histoire des franc-maçons.* Bruxelles: H.I.G. François, 1838.

Dufart, P. *Histoire de la fondation du Grand Orient de France.* Paris: L'imprimerie de Nouzou, rue de Clery, no. 9, 1812.

Durkheim, Émile. *The Elementary Forms of Religious Life.* London: George Allen & Unwin, 2008 [1912].

————. *The Rules of Sociological Method.* Glencoe: Free Press, 1966 [1895].

Eckhardt, Wolfgang. *The First Socialist Schism: Bakunin vs. Marx in the International Working Men's Association.* Oakland: PM Press, 2016.

Edelman, Nicole. "Somnabulisme, médiumnité et socialisme." *Politica Hermetica* 9 (1995).

Edwards, Stewart, and Elizabeth Fraser, ed. *Selected Writings of Pierre-Joseph Proudhon.* London: Macmillan, 1969.

Ehrenreich, Barbara, and Dierdre English. *Witches, Midwives and Nurses: A History of Women Healers.* New York: The Feminist Press, 1973.

Eisenstein, Elizabeth L. *The First Professional Revolutionist: Filippo Michele Buonarroti (1761–1837).* Cambridge, MA: Harvard University Press, 1959.

Eliade, Mircea. *The Myth of the Eternal Return: Or, Cosmos and History.* Princeton, NJ: Princeton University Press, 1974 [1949].

Engels, Friedrich. "Progress of Social Reform on the Continent." In *Karl Marx and Friedrich Engels: Collected Works.* Vol. 3. Edited by Robert C. Tucker, 392–408. New York: International Publishers, 1975.

Etienne, Mona, and Eleanor Leacock, ed. *Women and Colonization: Anthropological Perspectives.* New York: Praeger Publishers, 1980.

Evans, Kate. *Red Rosa: A Graphic Biography of Rosa Luxemburg.* New York: Verso Books, 2015.

Faggionato, Raffaella. *A Rosicrucian Utopia in Eighteenth Century Russia: The Masonic Circle of N.I. Novikov.* Netherlands: Springer, 2005.

Faivre, Antoine. *Theosophy, Imagination, Tradition: Studies in Western Esotericism.* Translated by Cristine Rhone. New York: State University of New York Press, 2000.

Farrow, Lynne. "Feminism as Anarchism." *Aurora* 4 (1974).

Federici, Silvia. *Caliban and the Witch: Women, the Body and Primitive Accumulation.* New York: Autonomedia, 2004.

Ferrer Benimeli, José Antonio. "La masonería española y la cuestion social." *Estudios de historia social* 40–41 (1987): 7–47.

Fortun, Kim. "Lone Gunmen: Legacies of the Gulf War, Illness, and Unseen Enemies." In Marcus, *Paranoia within Reason,* 343–74.

Fortun, Kim, and Micheal Fortun. "Due Diligence and the Pursuit of Transparency: The Securities and Exchange Commission, 1996." In Marcus, *Paranoia within Reason,* 157–96.

Foucault, Michel. *L'ordre du discours.* Paris: Gallimard, 2004.

La Franc-maçonne ou révélation des mystères des franc-maçons. Brussels: 1744.

Francovich, Carlo. "Gli illuminati di Weishaupt e l'idea egualitaria in alcune società segrete del Risorgimento." *Movimento Operaio* 4, no. 4 (1952): 553–97.

Fried, Albert, and Ronald Sanders. *Socialist Thought: A Documentary History.* New York: Anchor Books, 1964.

Gabay, Alfred J. *The Covert Enlightenment: Eighteenth-Century Counterculture and Its Aftermath.* West Chester, PA: Swedenborg Foundation Publishers, 2005.

Gay, Peter. *The Enlightenment: An Interpretation* New York: Knopf, 1966.

Gerth, H.H., and C. Wright Mills, ed. *From Max Weber: Essays in Sociology.* New York: Routledge, 2009.

González Fernández, Ángeles. "Masonería y modernización social: la transformacion del obrero en ciudadano (1868–1931)." *Bulletin d'histoire contemporaine de l'Espagne* 32–36 (2003): 89–116.

Goodrick-Clarke, Nicolas. *The Occult Roots of Nazism: Secret Aryan Cults and Their Influence on Nazi Ideology: The Ariosophists of Austria and Germany, 1890–1935.* New York: New York University Press, 1993.

Graeber, David. "The New Anarchists." *New Left Review* 13, January–February (2002): 61–74.

———. "Radical Alterity Is Just Another Way of Saying 'Reality': A Reply to Eduardo Viveiros De Castro." *Hau: Journal of Ethnographic Theory* 5, no. 2 (2015).

Gramsci, Antonio. *Selections from the Prison Notebooks of Antonio Gramsci.* Translated by Quintin Hoare and Geoffrey Nowell Smith. New York: International Publishers, 1971.

Hall, Stuart. "On Postmodernism and Articulation: An Interview with Stuart Hall (Edited by Lawrence Grossberg)." In *Stuart Hall: Critical Dialogues in Cultural Studies.* Edited by David Morley and Kuan-Hsing Chen. New York: Routledge, 1996.

Hart, John M. *Anarchism and the Mexican Working Class, 1860–1931.* Austin: University of Texas Press, 1978.

Harvey, Neil. *The Chiapas Rebellion: The Struggle for Land and Democracy.* Durham, NC: Duke University Press, 1998.

Heckethorn, Charles William. *The Secret Societies of All Ages and Countries.* Vol. 2. London: Bentley, 1875.

Hegel, Georg Wilhelm Friedrich. *Phenomenology of Spirit.* Translated by A.V. Miller. Oxford: Clarendon Press, 1977 [1807].

———. *The Science of Logic*. Translated by George Di Giovanni. Cambridge: Cambridge University Press, 2010 [1812].

Hellinger, Daniel. "Paranoia, Conspiracy, and Hegemony in American Politics." In *Transparency and Conspiracy*. Edited by Harry G. West and Todd Sanders, 204–32. Durham, NC: Duke University Press, 2003.

Hill, Christopher. *The World Turned Upside Down: Radical Ideas during the English Revolution*. Harmondsworth: Penguin Books, 1975.

Hobsbawm, E.J. *Primitive Rebels: Studies in Archaic Forms of Social Movement in the 19th and 20th Centuries*. New York: W.W. Norton & Co., 1959.

Hodges, Donald C. *Sandino's Communism: Spiritual Politics for the Twenty-First Century*. Austin: University of Texas Press, 1992.

Hofstadter, Richard. *The Paranoid Style in American Politics and Other Essays*. New York: Vintage Books, 2008.

Hull, Gloria, Patricia Bell Scott, and Barbara Smith, ed. *All the Women Are White, All the Blacks Are Men, but Some of Us Are Brave*. New York: The Feminist Press, 1982.

Hutton, Patrick. H. "The Art of Memory Reconceived: From Rhetoric to Psychoanalysis." *Journal of the History of Ideas* 48, no. 3 (1987): 371–92.

Icke, David. "Essential Knowledge for a Wall Street Protestor," October 21, 2011. Accessed July 20, 2018. https://www.youtube.com/watch?v=gV9A2IGShuk.

Illades, Carlos. *Rhodakanaty y la formación del pensamiento socialista en Mexico*. Rubi: Anthropos, 2002.

Israel, Jonathan. *Radical Enlightenment*. Oxford: Oxford University Press, 2001.

———. *A Revolution of Mind: Radical Enlightenment and the Intellectual Origins of Modern Democracy*. Princeton, NJ: Princeton University Press, 2010.

Jacob, Margaret C. "Freemasonry and the Utopian Impulse." In *Millenarianism and Messianism in English Literature and Thought*. Edited by R.H. Popkin. New York: E.J. Brill, 1988.

———. *The Radical Enlightenment: Pantheists, Freemasons and Republicans*. London: George Allen & Unwin, 1981.

———. *Strangers Nowhere in the World: The Rise of Cosmopolitanism in Early Modern Europe*. Philadelphia: University of Pennsylvania Press, 2006.

James, C.L. *Origin of Anarchism*. Chicago: A. Isaak, 1902.

Johnson, K., and K.E. Ferguson. "Anarchism and Indigeneity." In *The Palgrave Handbook of Anarchism*. Edited by Carl Levy and Matthew S. Adams. Basingstoke, UK: Palgrave Macmillan, 2019.

Jung, C.G. *Flying Saucers: A Modern Myth of Things Seen in the Skies*. Princeton, NJ: Princeton University Press, 1978.

Khasnabish, Alex. *Zapatismo Beyond Borders: New Imaginations of Political Possibility*. Toronto: University of Toronto Press, 2008.

Konishi, Sho. *Anarchist Modernity: Cooperatism and Japanese-Russian Intellectual Relations in Modern Japan*. Cambridge, MA: Harvard University Press, 2013.

———. "Reopening the 'Opening of Japan': A Russian-Japanese Revolutionary Encounter and the Vision of Anarchist Progress." *American Historical Review* 112, no. 1 (2007): 101–30.

Kornegger, Peggy. "Anarchism: The Feminist Connection." *The Second Wave* 4, no. 1 (1975).

Kropotkin, Peter. *Mutual Aid: A Factor of Evolution*. Boston: Extending Horizons Books, 1955 [1914].

Lacan, Jacques. *Écrits: The First Complete Edition in English*. Translated by Bruce Fink. New York: W.W. Norton & Co., 2006.

Lagalisse, Erica. "'Good Politics': Property, Intersectionality, and the Making of the Anarchist Self." PhD diss., McGill University, 2016.

———. "Gossip as Direct Action." In *Contesting Publics: Feminism, Activism, Ethnography*. Edited by Lynne Phillips and Sally Cole. London: Pluto Press, 2013.

———. "The Limits of 'Radical Democracy': A Gender Analysis of 'Anarchist' Activist Collectives in Montreal." *Altérités: Journal d'anthropologie du contemporain* 7, no. 1 (2010): 19–38.

———. "'Marginalizing Magdalena': Intersections of Gender and the Secular in Anarchoindigenist Solidarity Activism." *Signs: Journal of Women in Culture and Society* 36, no. 3 (2011).

———. "Occult Features of Anarchism." In *Essays on Anarchism and Religion*. Vol. 2, Edited by Alexandre Christoyannopoulos and Matthew Adams. Stockholm: Stockholm University Press, 2018.

———. "Participación e influencias anarquistas en el movimiento 'Occupy Wall Street.'" *Periodico del CNT (Confederación Nacional del Trabajo)* 383, (November 2011).

Lakoff, Aaron. *Anarchism and Hope*. Montréal: Howl! Arts Collective, 2013.

Lambert, Malcolm. *Medieval Heresy: Popular Movements from the Gregorian Reform to the Reformation*. Oxford: Basil Blackwell, 1992 [1977].

Laqueur, Thomas. "Why the Margins Matter: Occultism and the Making of Modernity." *Modern Intellectual History* 3, no. 1 (2006): 111–35.

Lauzeray, Christian. *L'Égypte ancienne et la franc-maçonnerie.* Paris: Éditeur Guy Trédaniel, 1988.

Le Forestier, René. *Les illuminés de Bavière et la franc-maçonnerie allemande.* Genève: Slatkine Megariotis Reprints, 1974 [1914].

Lea, Henry Charles. *A History of the Inquisition of the Middle Ages.* London: Macmillan, 1922.

Lehning, Arthur. *From Buonarroti to Bakunin: Studies in International Socialism.* Leiden: Brill, 1970.

———, ed. *Michael Bakunin: Selected Writings.* London: Johnathan Cape Ltd., 1973.

Lévi-Strauss, Claude. *Myth and Meaning.* London: Routledge, 2005 [1978].

Levy, Carl. Anarchism and Cosmopolitanism." *Journal of Political Ideologies* 16, no. 3 (2011): 265–78.

———. "Anarchism, Internationalism and Nationalism in Europe, 1860–1939." *Australian Journal of Politics and History* 50, no. 3 (2004): 330–42.

———. "Social Histories of Anarchism." *Journal for the Study of Radicalism* 4, no. 2 (2010): 1–44.

Levy, Richard S. *A Lie and a Libel: The History of the Protocols of the Elders of Zion.* Lincoln: University of Nebraska Press, 1995.

Lewis, Tyson, and Richard Kahn. "The Reptoid Hypothesis: Utopian and Dystopian Representational Motifs in David Icke's Alien Conspiracy Theory." *Utopian Studies* 16, no. 1 (2005): 45–74.

Lichtheim, George. *From Marx to Hegel.* New York: Herder and Herder, 1971.

Ligou, Daniel. "La franc-maçonnerie française au XVIII Siècle (positions des problèmes et état des questions)." *Information Historique* (1964).

Linebaugh, Peter, and Marcus Rediker. *The Many-Headed Hydra: Sailors, Slaves, Commoners, and the Hidden History of the Revolutionary Atlantic.* Boston: Beacon Press, 2000.

Lomnitz, Claudio. *The Return of Comrade Ricardo Flores Magón.* New York: Zone Books, 2014.

Magee, Glenn Alexander. *Hegel and the Hermetic Tradition.* Ithaca: Cornell University Press, 2001.

Manuel, Frank E., and Fritzie P. Manuel. *Utopian Thought in the Western World.* Cambridge, MA: Harvard University Press, 1979.

Marcus, George E. "Introduction to the Volume: The Paranoid Style Now." In Marcus, *Paranoia within Reason*, 1–12.

———, ed. *Paranoia within Reason: A Casebook on Conspiracy as Explanation*. Chicago: University of Chicago Press, 1999.

Marsden, Victor E., ed. *The Protocols of the Elders of Zion*. Las Vegas, NV: Filiquarian Publishing LLC, 2006.

Marshall, Peter. *Demanding the Impossible: A History of Anarchism*. London: Fontana Press, 1993.

Marx, Karl. *Capital*. Vol. 1. London: Penguin Books, 1990 [1876].

———. "The Eighteenth Brumaire of Louis Bonaparte." In *The Marx-Engels Reader*. Edited by Robert C. Tucker. New York: W.W. Norton & Co., 1978 [1852].

———. "The German Ideology." In Tucker, *The Marx-Engels Reader*.

Mehring, Franz. *Karl Marx: The Story of His Life*. Translated by Edward Fitzgerald. London: Allen & Unwin, 1936.

Moore, Henrietta. *Feminism and Anthropology*. Oxford: Polity Press, 1988.

Mornet, Daniel. *Les origines intellectuelles de la Révolution Française*. Paris: Librairie Armand Colin, 1933.

Mouffe, Chantal. "Hegemony and Ideology in Gramsci." In *Gramsci and Marxist Theory*. Edited by Chantal Mouffe, 168–204. London: Routledge, 1979.

Mounier, Jean Joseph. *On the Influence Attributed to Philosophers, Free-Masons, and to the Illuminati on the Revolution of France*. New York: Scholars' Facsimiles & Reprints, 1974 [1801].

Moya, Jose C. "The Positive Side of Stereotypes: Jewish Anarchists in Early Twentieth-Century Buenos Aires." *Jewish History* 18, no. 1 (2004): 19–48.

Mulsow, Martin. "Adam Weishaupt als Philosoph." In *Die Weimarer Klassik und ihre Geheimbünde*. Edited by Walter Müller-Seidel and Wolfgang Riedel. Würzburg: Königshausen und Neumann, 2003.

Nash, June. *Mayan Visions: The Quest for Autonomy in an Age of Globalization*. London: Routledge, 2001.

Nettlau, Max. *La anarquía a través de los tiempos*. Barcelona: Editorial Antalbe, 1979 [1929].

Notestein, Wallace. *A History of Witchcraft in England from 1558 to 1718*. New York: Thomas Y. Crowell Company, 1968.

Pagán, Victoria Emma. *Conspiracy Narratives in Roman History*. Austin: University of Texas Press, 2004.

———. *Conspiracy Theory in Latin Literature*. Austin: University of Texas Press, 2012.

———. "Toward a Model of Conspiracy Theory for Ancient Rome." *New German Critique* 35, no. 1 (2008).

Pelkmans, Mathijs, and Rhys Machold. "Conspiracy Theories and Their Truth Trajectories." *Focaal: Journal of Global and Historical Anthropology* 59 (2011): 66–80.

Pernicone, Nunzio. *Italian Anarchism, 1864–1892*. Princeton, NJ: Princeton University Press, 1993.

Pigden, Charles. "Popper Revisited, or, What Is Wrong with Conspiracy Theories?" *Philosophy of the Social Sciences* 25, no. 1 (1995): 3–34.

Pipes, Daniel. *The Hidden Hand: Middle Eastern Fears of Conspiracy*. New York: St. Martin's Griffin, 1998.

Polanyi, Karl. *The Great Transformation: The Political and Economic Origins of Our Time*. 2nd edition. Boston: Beacon Press, 2001 [1944].

Popper, Karl. "The Conspiracy Theory of Society." In *Conjectures and Refutations*. Edited by Karl Popper, 123–25. London: Routledge and Kegan Paul, 1963.

Preston, William. *The Universal Masonic Library, Vol. 3: Preston's Illustrations of Masonry*. New York: W. Leonard & Co., Aferican Masonic Agency, 1855.

Rafanelli, Leda. *I Belong Only to Myself: The Life and Writings of Leda Rafanelli*. Edited by Andrea Pakieser. Oakland: AK Press, 2014.

Reagon, Bernice Johnson. "Coalition Politics: Turning the Century." In *Home Girls: A Black Feminist Anthology*. Edited by Barbara Smith, 356–68. Latham, NY: Kitchen Table: Women of Color Press, 1983.

Riedel, Wolfgang. "Aufklärung und Macht: Schiller, Abel und die Illuminaten." In *Die Weimarer Klassik und ihre Geheimbünde*. Edited by Walter Müller-Seidel and Wolfgang Riedel. Würzburg: Königshausen und Neumann, 2003.

Roberts, J.M. *The Mythology of the Secret Societies*. London: Secker and Warburg, 1972.

Robison, John. *Proofs of a Conspiracy against All the Religions and Governments of Europe, Carried on in the Secret Meetings of Freemasons, Illuminati, and Reading Societies*. Dublin: W. Watson and Son, 1798.

Rose, R.B. *Gracchus Babeuf: The First Revolutionary Communist*. Stanford: Stanford University Press, 1978.

Rosenthal, Bernice Glatzer. Introduction to *The Occult in Russian and Soviet Culture*. Edited by Bernice Glatzer Rosenthal, 1–34. Ithaca: Cornell University Press, 1997.

———. "Political Implications of the Early Twentieth-Century Occult Revival." In Glatzer, *The Occult in Russian and Soviet Culture*, 379–418.

Rossi, Paulo. *Logic and the Art of Memory: The Quest for a Universal Language*. Chicago: University of Chicago Press, 2000.

Rublack, Ulinka. *The Astronomer and the Witch: Johannes Kepler's Fight for His Mother*. Oxford: Oxford University Press, 2015.

Sahlins, Marshall. "The Sadness of Sweetness: The Native Anthropology of Western Cosmology." *Current Anthropology* 37, no. 3 (1996): 395–428.

Said, Edward. *Orientalism*. New York: Vintage Books, 1978.

Saña, Heleno. *El anarquismo, de Proudhon a Cohn-Bendit*. Madrid: Indice, 1970.

Sanders, Todd, and Harry G. West. "Power Revealed and Concealed in the New World Order." In *Transparency and Conspiracy*. Edited by Harry West and Todd Sanders, 1–37. Durham, NC: Duke University Press, 2003.

Sandoval, Chela. "U.S. Third World Feminism: The Theory and Method of Oppositional Consciousness in the Postmodern World." *Genders* 10 (Spring 1991): 1–23.

Savigear, P. "Some Reflections on Corsican Secret Societies in the Early Nineteenth Century." *International Review of Social History* 19, no. 1 (1974): 100–14.

Schmitt, Carl. *Political Theology: Four Chapters on the Concept of Sovereignty*. Chicago: Chicago University Press, 1985 [1922].

Scholem, Gershom. *Major Trends in Jewish Mysticism*. Jerusalem: Schocken Publishing House, 1941.

Scott, Joan. "Sexularism." In *RSCAS Distinguished Lectures*. Florence, IT: European University Institute, Robert Schuman Institute for Advanced Studies, 2009.

Severi, Carlo. *The Chimera Principle: An Anthropology of Memory and Imagination*. Chicago: Hau, 2015.

Silverstein, Paul A. "An Excess of Truth: Violence, Conspiracy Theorizing, and the Algerian Civil War." *Anthropological Quarterly* 75, no. 4 (2002): 643–74.

Simpson, Audra. *Mohawk Interruptus: Political Life across the Borders of Settler States*. Durham, NC: Duke University Press, 2014.

Skeggs, Beverley. *Class, Self, Culture*. London: Routledge, 2004.

Smith, Andrea. *Conquest: Sexual Violence and American Indian Genocide*. Cambridge, MA: South End Press, 2005.

———. *North Americans and the Christian Right: The Gendered Politics of Unlikely Alliances*. Durham, NC: Duke University Press, 2008.

Spencer, Herbert. *Principles of Biology*. London: William and Norgate, 1864.

Spinoza, Benedictus de. *Ethics*. New York: Oxford University Press, 2000.

———. *Theological-Political Treatise*. Edited by Jonathan Israel. New York: Cambridge University Press, 2007.

Swami, Virin, and Adrian Furnham. "Political Paranoia and Conspiracy Theories." In *Power, Politics and Paranoia: Why People Are Suspicious of Their Leaders*. Edited by Jan-Willem van Prooijen and Paul A.M. van Lange. Cambridge: Cambridge University Press, 2014.

Szajkowski, Zosa. "The Jewish Saint-Simonians and Socialist Antisemites in France." *Jewish Social Studies* 9, no. 1 (1947): 33–60.

Tambiah, Stanley Jeyaraja. *Magic, Science, Religion and the Scope of Rationality*. Cambridge: Cambridge University Press, 1990.

Thomas, Keith. *Religion and the Decline of Magic: Studies in Popular Beliefs in Sixteenth- and Seventeenth-Century England*. New York: Penguin Books, 1982.

Thompson, E.P. *The Making of the English Working Class*. New York: Vintage Books, 1963.

Thory, Claude-Antoine. *Histoire de la fondation du Grand Orient de France*. Paris: l'Imprimerie de Nouzou, 1812.

Todd, Zoe. "An Indigenous Feminist's Take on the Ontological Turn: 'Ontology' Is Just Another Word for Colonialism." *Journal of Historical Sociology* 29, no. 1 (2016).

Tolstoy, Leo. "The Kingdom of God Is within You: Christianity Not as a Mystical Doctrine but as a New Understanding of Life." In *The Kingdom of God and Peace Essays*. New Delhi: Rupa & Co., 2001.

Tourniac, Jean. *Vie et perspectives de la franc-maçonnerie traditionelle*. 2nd ed. Paris: Dervy-Livres, 1978.

Trejo, Rubén. *Magonismo: utopia y revolucion, 1910–1913*. Mexico, DF: Cultura Libre, 2005.

Trevor-Roper, H.R. *The European Witch-Craze of the Sixteenth and Seventeenth Centuries*. Harmondsworth: Penguin Books, 1969.

Tsing, Anna. *The Mushroom at the End of the World: On the Possibility of Life in Capitalist Ruins*. Princeton, NJ: Princeton University Press, 2015.

———. "Unruly Edges: Mushrooms as Companion Species." *Environmental Humanities* 1 (2012): 141–54.

Valín Fernández, Alberto. "De masones y revolucionarios: una reflexión en torno e este encuentro." *Anuario Brigantino* 28 (2005): 173–98.

———. *Masonería y revolución: del mito literario a la realidad historica*. Santa Cruz de Tenerife: Ediciones Idea, 2008.

van der Veer, Peter. *Imperial Encounters: Religion and Modernity in India and Britain.* Princeton, NJ: Princeton University Press, 2001.

van Dülman, Richard. *Der Geheimbund der Illuminaten.* Stuttgart: Frommann-Holzboog Verlag, 1975.

Veysey, Laurence. *The Communal Experience: Anarchist and Mystical Counter-Cultures in America.* New York: Harper and Row, 1973.

Vondung, Klaus. "Millenarianism, Hermeticism, and the Search for a Universal Science." In *Science, Pseudoscience, and Utopianism in Early Modern Thought.* Edited by Stephen McKnight. Columbia, MO: University of Missouri Press, 1992.

Wakefield, Walter L., and Austin P. Evans. *Heresies of the High Middle Ages.* New York: Columbia University Press, 1991.

Webb, James. *The Occult Establishment.* La Salle, IL: Open Court Publishing Company, 1976.

Webster, Nesta H. *Secret Societies and Subversive Movements.* London: Boswell Printing and Publishing Co., 1936.

Westcott, Dr. William Wynn. *A Catalogue Raisonné of Works on the Occult Sciences, Vol. 3: Freemasonry, a Catalogue of Lodge Histories (England), with a Preface.* London: F.L. Gardner, 1912.

Westfall, Richard S. "Newton and the Hermetic Tradition." In *Science, Medicine and Society in the Renaissance: Essays to Honor Walter Pagel.* Edited by Allen G. Debus. New York: Science History Publications, 1972.

Woodcock, George. *Anarchism: A History of Libertarian Ideas and Movements.* Cleveland: The World Publishing Company, 1962.

Yates, Frances. *The Art of Memory.* London: Routledge, 1966.

———. *Giordano Bruno and the Hermetic Tradition.* Chicago: University of Chicago Press, 1964.

———. *The Rosicrucian Enlightenment.* London: Routledge, 2002 [1972].

Index

Page numbers in *italic* refer to illustrations. "Passim" (literally "scattered") indicates intermittent discussion of a topic over a cluster of pages.

About the Authors

Erica Lagalisse

Erica Lagalisse is a postdoctoral fellow at the London School of Economics (LSE) International Inequalities Institute, under the supervision of Dr. Beverley Skeggs. Her current research projects include a study of frictions surrounding "conspiracy theory" in social movement spaces, with the purpose of contributing constructive pedagogy around "conspiracy theory" as both an academic object and practical political problematic.

Lagalisse completed her PhD in Anthropology at McGill University in Montreal, Canada, during which time she held a visiting researcher appointment at the Centro de Investigaciones y Estudios Superiores en Antropologia Social (CIESAS) in Oaxaca, Mexico, and a U.S.-Canada Fulbright Fellowship at the Teresa Lozano Long Institute of Latin American Studies (LLILAS), at the University of Texas at Austin.

Lagalisse's doctoral thesis, *"Good Politics": Property, Intersectionality, and the Making of the Anarchist Self* (2016), explores anarchist networks that cross Québec, the United States, and Mexico to examine contradictions within solidarity activism and settler "anarchoindigenism." The work throws into relief the particular practices of university-educated Anglo-American leftists, and draws on anthropological, feminist, and critical race theory to show how they have preempted the black feminist challenge of "intersectionality" by recuperating its praxis within the logic of neoliberal self-making projects and property relations.

Barbara Ehrenreich

Barbara Ehrenreich is an author, essayist, and activist. Her twenty-two books to date include *Nickel and Dimed: On (Not) Getting by in America* and, most recently, *Natural Causes: An Epidemic of Wellness, the Certainty of Dying, and Killing Ourselves to Live Longer*.

ABOUT PM PRESS

PM Press was founded at the end of 2007 by a small collection of folks with decades of publishing, media, and organizing experience. PM Press co-conspirators have published and distributed hundreds of books, pamphlets, CDs, and DVDs. Members of PM have founded enduring book fairs, spearheaded victorious tenant organizing campaigns, and worked closely with bookstores, academic conferences, and even rock bands to deliver political and challenging ideas to all walks of life. We're old enough to know what we're doing and young enough to know what's at stake.

We seek to create radical and stimulating fiction and nonfiction books, pamphlets, T-shirts, visual and audio materials to entertain, educate, and inspire you. We aim to distribute these through every available channel with every available technology—whether that means you are seeing anarchist classics at our bookfair stalls, reading our latest vegan cookbook at the café, downloading geeky fiction e-books, or digging new music and timely videos from our website.

PM Press is always on the lookout for talented and skilled volunteers, artists, activists, and writers to work with. If you have a great idea for a project or can contribute in some way, please get in touch.

PM Press
PO Box 23912
Oakland, CA 94623
www.pmpress.org

PM Press in Europe
europe@pmpress.org
www.pmpress.org.uk

FRIENDS OF PM PRESS

These are indisputably momentous times—the
financial system is melting down globally and
the Empire is stumbling. Now more than ever
there is a vital need for radical ideas.

In the years since its founding—and on a
mere shoestring—PM Press has risen to the formidable challenge
of publishing and distributing knowledge and entertainment for the
struggles ahead. With over 300 releases to date, we have published an
impressive and stimulating array of literature, art, music, politics, and
culture. Using every available medium, we've succeeded in connecting
those hungry for ideas and information to those putting them into
practice.

Friends of PM allows you to directly help impact, amplify, and revitalize
the discourse and actions of radical writers, filmmakers, and artists. It
provides us with a stable foundation from which we can build upon our
early successes and provides a much-needed subsidy for the materials
that can't necessarily pay their own way. You can help make that
happen—and receive every new title automatically delivered to your
door once a month—by joining as a Friend of PM Press. And, we'll throw
in a free T-shirt when you sign up.

Here are your options:

• **$30 a month** Get all books and pamphlets plus 50% discount on all
  webstore purchases

• **$40 a month** Get all PM Press releases (including CDs and DVDs)
  plus 50% discount on all webstore purchases

• **$100 a month** Superstar—Everything plus PM merchandise, free
  downloads, and 50% discount on all webstore purchases

For those who can't afford $30 or more a month, we have **Sustainer
Rates** at $15, $10 and $5. Sustainers get a free PM Press T-shirt and a
50% discount on all purchases from our website.

Your Visa or Mastercard will be billed once a month, until you tell us to
stop. Or until our efforts succeed in bringing the revolution around. Or
the financial meltdown of Capital makes plastic redundant. Whichever
comes first.